Confident Leadership In 21st Century Business:

Bridging the Generation Gaps

By Rosemarie Barnes

Publisher: MBK Enterprises, LLC
Publication Date: 2017
©2017 by Rosemarie Barnes   All Rights Reserved
Printed in USA

ISBN 10: 0-9971687-6-5
ISBN 13: 978-0-9971687-6-1

Edited by: Jay Polmar - Speed Read America
Design, Layout and Graphics by Becky Norwood
Cover Design by: Angie Ayala

T hank you to the many individuals who agreed to speak with me about the challenges and benefits of leading multigenerational workplaces. Thank you for your candor and for your understanding that bridging the generation gaps in business is a vitally important part of today's leadership responsibilities.

Rosemarie Barnes

Table of Contents

Introduction 7

Chapter 1: Understanding Leadership 9

    Definition and Clarification 10

    Critical Business Leadership Skills........................... 13

    The Power of Values 23

    Communication Skills... 26

Chapter 2: Understanding Generational Differences 35

    In Praise of Generation X, Y, and Z 40

    Generational Synopses 43

    Characteristics... 71

    Rationale 73

    Work Expectations 75

    Maslow's Hierarchy of Needs Applied to
    Employee Engagement 78

    The Rise of Women in the Workplace.................... 81

    The Dopamine Effect & the Rise of the
    Helicopter Parent.. 84

    Generational Needs 87

Special Needs in Business 99

In a Nutshell 103

Summary 106

Chapter 3: Disruption Leadership **107**

Nudge Theory 109

Laws of Persuasion 112

Change Leadership 132

Work Cultures 134

Charisma 139

Communicating with your Team 143

Outcome Based Thinking 148

Reactionary vs. Proactive Change Response 149

Conclusion **151**

Introduction

A good leader inspires people to have confidence in him. A great leader inspires people to have confidence in themselves.

~Lao Tzu

Business leaders are becoming increasingly frustrated by the changing attitudes of today's employees. Not only do leaders and managers need to keep on top of rapid technological advances, but today's job seekers are changing the very face of how business is conducted.

Using gross generalities only to make a point, the Millennials are brilliant, but are also seen as entitled, and with no internal motivation. Generation Z, the latest to begin to hit the job market and with tremendous knowledge and technological astuteness, will not abide the pyramidal corporate structures so common in the past. How can the immense combined power of these groups of individuals be harnessed for the success of a company?

Being a leader in today's business world is a little bit like being a ringleader in a circus. To be successful, the circus ringleader needs to supply the lion tamers with a chair and a whip, the trapeze artists require their swings and a net, and the trick riders must have their horses and special saddles. Similarly, in business the good leader is aware that

Generation X prefers carefully funneled information, Generation Y feeds on mentorship and praise, and the upcoming Generation Z needs to understand how their tasks fit in with the whole.

In this new age, the role of leader has also changed. What qualifies an individual as a leader today? Is it the role they play? Is it the skills they bring? Is it their title?

Great leaders don't always have the role of, "the boss," and they're not always the bossy ones, either. Leaders arise out of ordinary circumstances and in all age groups. There are leaders on the playground, on work crews, in offices, on boards, and even in retirement homes. There are natural leaders, and there are those who have learned the skills. True leaders are not bullies ruling through power and fear. They have no need for coercion or deception. They inspire others to greatness, and are not threatened by the accomplishments of others. This has neverchanged.

What about in business? What skills and attributes do great business leaders possess that encourage the executives, managers, supervisors, and employees of today's hugely diverse workforce to jointly contribute to the success of a company and at the same time provide opportunities and support for these same individuals to become innovators and leaders themselves?

The 20th century version of leadership has all but disappeared and leaders are reeling, not knowing how to bridge the huge generation gaps in business today.

CHAPTER 1

Understanding Leadership

"Being a leader at work is important, but our world needs leaders at all levels, as well. We need people who can inspire others, who can rally people of different talents to solve problems, and who are willing to share responsibility and see other points of view."

~Robert E. Moritz, US Chairman and Senior Partner at PricewaterhouseCoopers

DEFINITION AND CLARIFICATION

Leadership:

Self-confidence is the fundamental basis from which leadership grows.

Confidence grows from self-awareness.

Therefore, the key to sustainable leadership is self-awareness.

Without confidence, there is no leadership

What leadership is not:

Leadership has nothing to do with seniority or one's position in the hierarchy of a company.

Leadership has nothing to do with titles.

Leadership has nothing to do with personal attributes.

Leadership is not management.

Leadership vs. Management

The first item for clarification is the difference between Leadership and Management and the union between them.

Management:

The authority granted to an individual by an organization.

Leadership:

The authority granted to an individual by their followers.

Management is about maintaining processes, disciplines, and systems. Where managers keep the rules, leaders have to be willing to break them, or at least find creative ways around them. Leaders must have vision, creativity, and the ability to influence others to follow and support them into uncharted and often risky territory. All leaders should encourage others around them to rise to the challenge and become leaders themselves. The business world needs both managers and leaders to fill the role of the, "boss."

~ Richard Branson, Virgin Group

Leadership is only effective when management is efficient. They must go hand in hand.

~ Alex Ihama

Effective leadership is putting first things first. Effective management is discipline, carrying it out.

~ Stephen Covey

Management is efficiency in climbing the ladder of success; leadership determines whether the ladder is leaning against the right wall.

~ Stephen Covey

Management is doing things right; leadership is doing the right things.

~ Peter Drucker

Some individuals are leaders even when in a position of management, and some are managers even when in a leadership situation. Larger companies have the luxury of both positions; smaller companies and entre- or solo-preneurs may need to wear both hats. It is important to recognize when managerial responsibilities begin to force out the leadership role just as it is equally important to fulfill your management role even while you are knee-deep in the leadership process. The skills of the two roles may overlap in a number of instances, but when one or the other of the roles is missing, the effects are keenly felt throughout the company.

The question asked by today's people of business is, whether the essence of the roles of leadership and management have endured the test of time, or whether they have evolved through desire or necessity.

LEADERSHIP	MANAGEMENT
About the overall goal	About the associated objectives
About the people	About the process
Sustained by contagious passion	Sustained by commanding procedures
Attracts people	Helps people support the vision
Subjective	Objective
Initiates	Mitigates
Consistently inspires	Consistently informs
Proposes	Facilitates
Innovates	Renovates
Listens	Speaks
Focuses on the purpose	Focuses on the planning
Generates the excitement	Accelerates the execution

CRITICAL BUSINESS LEADERSHIP SKILLS

Don't tell people how to do things. Tell them what to do and let them surprise you with their results.

~ George S. Patton Jr

Business Leadership champions a greater cause, a noble vision, an aim or objective for the benefit of the business, its people, and in the greater sense, humanity.

Leaders:

- Engage in conversations that unlock possibilities that brings out the best in individuals,
- Show up in powerful moods such as ambition, gratitude, joy, and wonder that brings out more of these good moods in others,
- Show up open, relaxed, and centered, keeping themselves present in the current conversation.

Is this a change? Is this a change in the world of politics, the military, business, and social circles or in family circles? Leaders are found everywhere. Here, of course we are examining the vital skills in the world of business, but there is a body of constants that leaders display almost universally.

What then, are the continuing skills of leadership?

Consider the validity of these statements as they pertain to critical business leadership skills.

Warning: these are not as easy as they appear.

- Focus on relationships not facts.

- Add value by enabling things to happen, not by doing the work.
- Practice seeing the bigger picture, not mastering the details.
- Rely on, "executive presence," to project confidence, not on having all the facts or answers.

Page after page and article after article purports expertise in discovering, aligning, and distilling the attributes of great leaders. Insight has been offered in different forms and fashions over the years. Consider the following two examples taken from two different eras:

Sample #1

Fortitude: Mental and emotional strength in facing difficulty, adversity, danger, or temptation courageously; the strength of mind along with physical and moral courage to persevere in the face of adversity.

Temperance/Responsibility: Self-discipline to control passions and appetites; being accountable, pursuing excellence, exercising self-restraint in action, statement; self-control.

Prudence: Practical wisdom and the ability to make the right choice in specific situations.

Justice/Fairness: Honesty, lawfulness, keeping promises; adherence to a balanced standard of justice without relevance to one's own feeling or inclinations.

Trustworthiness: Deserving of trust or confidence, dependable, reliable; honesty, integrity, loyalty; refraining from deception.

Respect: Behavior toward others; civility, courtesy, decency, dignity, autonomy, tolerance, and acceptance; the prohibition of humiliation, manipulation, and exploitation.

Caring: Honest expressions of benevolence and altruism.

Sample #2

Do Not boast, brag, bully, or polarize: Old school leadership was egocentric and narcissistic. To change meant he/she had somehow, inconceivably, made a mistake.

Do Not avoid the real issues: Today's employees are smart, tech savvy, and informed. Dodging the real issues leads to distrust and contempt.

Do Not throw your peers or the current leader under the bus: Leadership and management must present a unified front and actively model appropriate behavior so that employees are reassured and less change resistance.

Do Not make promises that you know you cannot keep: The most beloved leaders are those who stand by what they say, walk the walk, and talk the talk. Not keeping promises is the precursor to career and business failure.

Do Not ignore the elephant in the room: Deal with the issues. Discuss the controversy. Address the real unspoken issues, and then invite dialogue and problem solving action plans.

Do Not only focus on the big picture: It's important, but the best leaders know that it is equally important to outline small, measurable goals for people to attain along the way. Smaller milestones also create check points along the way to the ultimate destination.

Do Not micro manage: Smart delegation communicates your trust to the team, and allows them to grow and develop. Heavy handed management always causes tension.

Do Not forget to applaud small wins: Every big win is an accumulation of a series of smaller wins. Research shows that meaningful recognition is the #1 thing that empowers others to do great things.

Do Not under-value good communication: Leaders who are good communicators (clear messages, transparency, and open door policy) inspire action and innovation, and foster the kind of teamwork and creativity that drives results.

Do Not set yourself apart: Show your group that you are part of the team and great things start to happen. The first step is leading by example showing that teamwork and camaraderie are priorities.

Do Not discourage innovation: Give people room to tinker, try things out, and make mistakes. Be sure your team knows which projects with which they can take some time and try out new solutions. Be supportive of the occasional failure; your team will know you've got their backs, and will be equally supportive of you.

Do Not forget to celebrate milestones: Birthdays and work anniversaries are important occasions to celebrate and appreciate your co-workers. Employees of all generations agree.

A noteworthy difference between the two samples is the perspective. Notice that the air of the first example places the leader above the status of the employees. This is not at all surprising given that when the piece was written, businesses were completely hierarchical with the chain of command being concise and expected. It was the pyramid, with the leader at the top, a couple of top advisers, a few upper management, more middle management, even more entry-level managers, and so on down to the base of the pyramid where the masses of employees worked.

The attributes of a leader in the first instance speak of benevolence and altruism, of dignity, tolerance, and the prohibition of humiliation and exploitation. It speaks of physical and moral courage, and deserving of trust. It was written from an egocentric point of view, and clearly demanded that leaders behave in a god-like fashion in order that commands be accepted as fair and just, and therefore, obeyed without complaint. It was written from an untouchable and majestic ruler's point of view.

However, there is nothing untrue about the content. The tenets hold just as well today as they did when written and bear close attention not only by leaders but by every single human being.

The second example is very clearly written much more recently. Note the use of more common language, and colloquialisms, e.g. "throw your peers or the current leaders under the bus."

Teamwork, cooperation, and collaboration play an important role in defining positive leadership qualities, whereas there was no hint of those attributes in the first sample. Where the first definition placed leaders above employees, the second has a complete category for, "Do not set yourself apart." It speaks about celebrating employee birthdays, and addresses the failure of "heavy-handed management." It speaks to fulfilling the personal and professional needs of the employees. It displays a completely different attitude between leader and employee. Again, there is nothing untrue or irrelevant in this example and again merits attention.

But, what if it isn't an either/or decision? What if an ideal avatar of leadership isn't possible because of hugely diverse industries, employee needs, and business models? Today's workforce is demanding individual attention and leaders are being forced to reckon with the realization that a one-sized-fits-all leadership style is no longer as effective as it once might have been.

Let's have a look at 2 more examples from the 21st century:

Only focusing on the big picture: It's true, great leaders communicate the big picture vision. It's how they inspire people to strive for goals that are far off into the future, or still somewhat vague. But the best leaders also know that it's a rookie mistake to fail to outline small goals for their people to achieve along the way.

Not delegating the work: This one's a classic. Everyone's had at least one micro-managing boss who is overly absorbed in small details and too controlling to allow team members to take the reins.

Failing to applaud small wins: Every big win is an accumulation of many smaller win, so why would you let those everyday successes slip by unnoticed? Keep a stack of cards at your desk so you can write a thank-you note when someone goes above and beyond for you.

Communicating poorly: Wordy emails, lack of transparency and oversight, not having an open-door policy, these are all surefire ways to be a bad communicator.

Setting yourself apart: The worst leaders are the ones who believe they're better than everyone else...and they don't bother to hide it. To avoid giving this impression, take the time to get to know teammates.

Discouraging innovation: Maybe you try to be supportive of creativity, or you encourage team members to weigh in on important decisions. You may think that you're fostering innovation. But if you're not giving people room to tinker, try things out, and make mistakes, then you're not really opening the door to true innovation.

Forgetting to celebrate the milestones: 21st Century professionals often have hectic schedules, and you may think it's not a big deal to forget a birthday or work anniversary here or there. But it is. In fact, it's inexcusable, especially given the whole suite of organizational tools and apps you can use for reminders.

(Taken from Sturt and Nordstrom, "7 Leadership Mistakes to Avoid in 2016)

Compare that one to this:

Establish trust: Step 1 to establishing trust is through transparency. Transparency breeds trust, which in turn breeds engagement, whether with your employees, your board, or your clients. Transparent leaders and organizations are successful because they are trusted.

Be clear: Making decisions based within corporate and personal values and be accountable for them. Announcing decisions using consistent language and applying those decisions within a consistent system lets everyone know the rules of the game and that apply to everything and everyone within the company.

Keep lines of communication open: It is vital to ask for and receive feedback, anonymously if necessary, and to respond to what you hear. It is equally important to bravely broach controversial topics and not allow the rumor mill to be churning up uncertainty. Good news or bad is best heard from the leaders, and not from the newspapers or a client.

Focus on why, not what: Employees need to know how their work fits into the organization. If we know the why of the decision, we are more likely to participate in the what. Creating a participatory environment involves everyone and decisions are not made solely from the top down. Honesty and transparency from the leaders breeds the same in return from the employees.

Mary Kelly wrote an article about the goal of leadership wherein she spoke of the responsibility of leadership to:

Do our best to make sure that people are motivated, focused, and optimistic about possibilities, even when updates or industry forecasts look bleak.

Be optimistic. People watch what you do, how you respond, and your mannerisms. If you are not genuinely optimistic, your people will see right through you.

Leaders should focus on their employees. Meet with employees to discuss their careers, training programs, attending conferences, and increasing responsibilities so that they are eligible for future opportunities.

She went on to share the following thoughts with other leaders:

Don't complain to your team or your customers. Great bosses learn not to complain in front of their people, even when they have something to complain about.

Ask probing, open-ended questions to find out what is really going on.

Ask questions that inspire answers with substance, such as:

- "What are you working on right now?"
- "Is there anything you think we do here that wastes time?
- "Can you think of ways we can decrease frustration?"
- "What can we provide that would help you do your job better?"
- "What do you think senior leadership should know?"

Watch for crises.

- Managers also need to make sure that employees know that help and friends are available in the event of depression or other issues.

- Give employees the gift of your time. Especially during the busiest times, it clearly demonstrates your caring, and relieves much of their stress.

The Soldiers and the Trench

The story goes that sometime, close to a battlefield over 200 years ago, a man in civilian clothes rode past a small group of exhausted battle-weary soldiers digging an obviously important defensive position. The section leader, making no effort to help, was shouting orders, threatening punishment if the work was not completed within the hour.

"Why are you are not helping?" asked the stranger on horseback.

"I am in charge. The men do as I tell them," said the section leader, adding, "Help them yourself if you feel strongly about it."

To the section leader's surprise the stranger dismounted and helped the men until the job was finished.

Before leaving the stranger congratulated the men for their work, and approached the puzzled section leader.

"You should notify top command next time your rank prevents you from supporting your men - and I will provide a more permanent solution," said the stranger.

Up close, the section leader now recognized General Washington and the lesson he'd just been taught.

(This story is allegedly based on truth. Similar examples are found in history, and arise in modern times too, so please forgive the mythical possibility of the above attribution; the story's message is more important than its historical accuracy.)

The reason George Washington was a great leader was that his primary interest was to support his men as they fought to fulfill the ideal.

George led through **Outcome Based Thinking,** (see Chapter 3) as all great leaders do; he just didn't know the name of what he was doing. After deliberating and making a decision about what he wanted, he created a game plan, a strategy to reach that end.

In the instance of the little parable just cited, he needed a strong defensive position and clearly saw what needed to be done to accomplish it. To get the job done, his men needed help, so as the leader, he provided that help in whatever form was needed; in this case through his own physical work digging the defensive position. The section leader thought his power came through command and control. George Washington's power came through true leadership.

THE POWER OF VALUES

When your values are clear to you,
making decisions becomes easier.

~Roy E. Disney

Every business leader must know their own capabilities, and to do that, they must first know who they are: theirs values, their passions, the culture they wish to build, and to what lengths they will go to achieve the desired outcome.

In 2015, Alaina Love wrote that for leaders to shoulder their enormous responsibilities to their company, to their staff, and to their legacy, they first need to know who they are, what their passions are, how they impact others, and what their boundaries are. These are not light questions answerable with off-hand responses. She continues:

1. Who am I?

This is more than a "name, rank and serial number" kind of question. Knowing who you are means you deeply understand why you're here and the unique contributions you intend to make — not just to the organization, but also to the larger world. It means having a profound sense of purpose in your life and the capacity to articulate it well, so that you engage and inspire others. You should be able to fill in the blank in the sentence "My purpose in life is to _____."

If you can't, it's time to start working towards that answer, because your success as a leader depends upon it. Authentic leaders can visualize the sight line between their own purpose and the mission of the organization to such a profound degree that their work is more than a job, it's an extension of who they are.

2. What are my passions?

This is not a question that seeks to understand if you're passionate about food, wine, football, or skydiving, nor if you're passionate about that attractive new member of your tennis club. The understanding of passion that's essential for you to lead well requires deep insight into the passions that you express as a result of the purpose that drives you.

After years of working with leaders around the globe, significant research has revealed 10 core passions that operate in everyone. They are codified as the following passion archetypes: Builder, Transformer, Teacher, Connector, Healer, Altruist, Conceiver, Creator, Processor, and Discoverer.

Knowing that you are a passionate Builder, for example, will drive you to achieve huge goals and dream big dreams. But, if you are managing someone with a Processor passion, you'll need to slow down and lay out a detailed plan if you want to gain their support and benefit from their expertise. Understanding your own passions and how they interplay with those of others empowers you to leverage both the skills and the passions of the people on your team to get the best results.

3. How am I impacting others?

As a leader, a critical responsibility is to design and maintain the culture of the organization. If your people debate and discuss issues openly and then work together to arrive at the best path forward, it's because you've created a culture where information-hoarding is frowned upon and where people are encouraged to take risk and explore new ideas.

Conversely, if your culture is one that pushes against reality and demands, rather than inspires results, you're likely to have few people around you who commit to your vision or tell you when the data proves that it's flawed.

4. Where are my edges?

Knowing the boundaries of your value system and clearly understanding what you're not willing to do to win favor or profit provides you with an internal GPS to guide your behaviors. In the safety of our own thoughts, it's easy to define ourselves as we'd like others to see us, but the work environment is where all those perceptions get tested. It's where you are challenged to demonstrate the courage of your convictions as a leader and where you learn to embrace both your strengths and your weaknesses.

Knowing your edges will prompt you to ask important questions of the business and the decisions that are made by you and other leaders in it. Beyond the question "Is what we're planning to do legal?" a strong value system will cause you to ask, "Is this the right thing to do for our business and the promise of our brand?"

Our values are the key to leadership, and they guide our leadership styles. Every great leader spends substantial time discovering and uncovering her/her core values, and then continually monitors them for changes. Our beliefs do change over time as we gain more knowledge, experience, and applications; if we don't know what we believe today, how can we be assured our goals are still worthy?

Further, we must absolutely know our desired goal, else how can we possibly chart an effective and efficient route to get there?

Additionally, if we don't have a firm commitment to reaching that goal, how can we persuade others to join us in our pursuit? Now add the generation gaps in business, coupled with the changing motivations of the new workforce, and we find our former leadership styles and techniques are no longer effective. Working harder and becoming even more firm in our dedication is not enough to reach our own personal goals or that of our companies.

Leaders are faced with creating and choosing possibilities and paths, making decisions that can affect the entire business and its people, fulfilling the need to continually inspire and motivate others both inside and beyond the walls of the business. He/she must be perceived as confident but not arrogant, bendable but not breakable, responsive instead of reactive. The secret to making it all look easy and secure is for the leader to live his/her values and let them be the guide when all else becomes chaos.

COMMUNICATION SKILLS

It is impossible to overstress the importance of communication skills for leaders. Of the plethora of talents, skills, and aptitudes necessary for great leadership, the value of communication trumps them all. After all, an idea remains only an idea unless action follows, and without brilliantly sharing it with all parties, in the language they need to hear, no action will ever occur. The idea dies before it can even take root.

During the ages of command and control leadership, communication skills still played an enormous role, but because of the tendency of the workforce to obey commands without question, persuasion was not as vital as it is today.

Asking, "Why?" would have been outrageous in the middle of the 20th century, whereas today, leaders must adapt to expect the question. This is one of the most common complaints current business leaders have: the workforce is demanding to know the "whys" of every request.

There's a disconnection between the "boss" expecting the commands to be completed, and the employees wanting to understand the reasons for the request. The former tends to feel threatened by the questioning while the latter believe that if they know the "why" they can do a better job. It comes down to a communication issue and an understanding of the amount of information to share.

Business leaders are, for the most part, living under the false illusion that they can speak to their colleagues, counterparts, and employees the same way they speak to others. This one mistake causes more damage than they know. Leaders (and anyone who represents the business by speaking of it) must accept that when they say even one single word about their business, no matter to whom, they are speaking in public.

Public speaking is an art form in and of itself, and requires dedicated study and practice to be done well. The benefits of speaking well are immense, as are, unfortunately, the negative results of doing it poorly. Whether one to one, one to a few, or one to many, speaking of business must be handled with finesse, be designed to address the listener's top of mind problem, and always answer their burning questions of, "What's in it for me?" and, "How does this affect me?"

Language:

- Is the fundamental tool of a human being and a leader, and
- The quality of conversations determines the quality of results from your people.

Do you...

- Engage in conversations that unlock possibility that brings out the best in individuals and allow them to participate fully and freely in conversation?

Or do you...

- Engage in conversation that shuts out possibilities for others and stifle any potential for success and engagement?

Moods and Emotions:

- We cannot escape our moods and emotions
- To show up as a leader we must understand how emotions create an environment where individuals thrive.

Do you...

- Show up in powerful moods such as ambition, gratitude, joy, and wonder that bring out more of these good moods in others?

Or do you...

- Live in moods such as resignation, resentment, anxiety, or frustration that cause others to dismiss or avoid you because of the negativity?

The Body:

- Is more than a vessel to transport your brain from task to task
- Is a complex system designed to convert moods and emotions and determine what conversations might show up

Do you...

- Show up in an open, relaxed, and centered form, keeping you present in the current conversation?

Or do you...

- Show up stiff and stoic, leaving you only as a brain on a stick, leaving you unable to tap into its wisdom to connect with your followers?

The topic of excellent speaking skills is another book all by itself, and happily, one is available to you. **Confident Public Speaking: Being Heard Above the Noise has** been reviewed as an excellent text book for learning the essential skills for speaking of business. It's a very good book; I know because I wrote it!

In all sincerity, the value of honed and practiced speaking skills is tremendous, and will allow you to persuade, inspire, and engage your employees and audiences much more effectively. Leaders must reach excellence in so many areas, and speaking and communication skills must rightfully be placed at the top of the list.

The following list, taken from social media, cites the 12 of the most-complained-about speaking habits of Millennials and has been included here for your entertainment, and for comparison to your own speaking characteristics:

1. Saying things like: "It seems like my time would be best spent..."

"This person sounds responsible, but they've potentially ditched the team's goals and priorities for their own preferences. They want to do what they want to do, but what if they are missing the whole point of owning the big picture and what's needed? Maybe, truthfully, they think they just can't do it."

Andy Hooper - Vice President - Gap International

2. "I can't even."

"This sarcastic phrase indicating a breaking point or speechlessness is entirely overused and can undermine the speaker's professionalism. What is acceptable in a casual meeting at the coffee shop may not be well received by co-workers from an older generation."

Katie Kern - PR and Marketing Director - Media Frenzy Global

3. "Like..."

"As a Millennial myself, I can tell you the biggest thing my generation needs to get rid of is using the word 'like' with such excessiveness.   There is nothing that will (lead you to being) dismissed more quickly than a few too many 'likes' during a meeting or on a call."

Peter Mertens – Associate - Burson-Marsteller

4. "Literally."

"We literally need to stop overusing literally. It's literally useless to toss it in every sentence. We literally don't recognize that we're abusing the literal meaning of the word. Fellow Millennials, please join me in banning the word from our vocabulary. I'm literally begging you."

Greg Rudolph - Founder and CEO-BoardBlazers.com

5. "Man."

"One of the most common habits I've noticed [among] Millennials (including myself) is using the word 'man' in sentences, making them sound less professional: 'All right man, that sounds good.' ... In many cases it just comes across as unprofessional. Honestly, I have this habit and it's something I'm trying to break."

Brandon Howard – Owner - All My Web Needs

6. "Dude."

"A lot of Millennials like to use the word 'dude' when they're in a professional setting. Many older professionals won't take you seriously if you use the word dude as it is too casual and makes you sound immature."

Michelle Kop - Marketing Specialist -GMR Transcription

7. "Yeah, yeah, yeah..."

"Yeah, yeah, yeah," (suggesting that the listener wants the speaker to hurry up and finish so that he or she can speak.) It's important for Millennials to demonstrate to older generations that they are active listeners. At its worst, this may make them come off as a know-it-all with a short attention span."

Brandon Shockley
- Qualitative Researcher and Marketing Strategist - Plannerzone, Inc.

8. "Yup."

"I often receive replies from young people that say, 'ya,' 'yah,' or 'yup.' I have had written correspondence, particularly in email, with this one word as a reply. I'm not alone. Many professionals cringe at this response. It feels overly familiar, lazy, and disrespectful. Especially, when 'yes' takes the same amount of time to type as 'yah' or 'yup.' "

Lida Citroen – Principal - Lida 360

9. Speaking with a rising tone of voice.

"Practice having an authoritative tone which tends to go down a third of an octave at the end of a sentence in which you want to make a point. That unconsciously communicates your taking a stance and also something you stand for to other people."

Mark Goulston - Founder and Co-CEO - The Goulston Group

10. Making not-really-an-excuse excuses.

"Examples: 'I'm sorry I'm late, my cross-fit class was so hard this morning and I needed some extra recovery time.'
Or: 'I know the project was due yesterday but I was at a charity event last night and ate something bad and wasn't feeling so well this morning.' "

Christine DiDonato - Founder, Career Revolution Inc.

11. Over sharing (the wrong things).

"I've had Millennial clients say, 'I never had a college internship because I was too busy playing soccer, and now I can't get a job.' But, it turns out that they had a sports scholarship, and made Dean's List all four years and were close to going pro. When I ask if they tell interviewers all that, they look surprised: 'Um, no... Why? Should I?'"

Carlota Zimmerman - Career Coach - Carolota World Wide

12. Talking too fast.

"Young people often want to prove themselves, [and they] speak fast so they get heard at all. They need to slow down. For all ages the rule of thumb is: The more time you give yourself, the more status people give you."

Debra Benton, Executive Coach

It seems that our world is becoming more casual. Can you imagine what the businessmen of Victorian England would think of men going to work in the clothes we now wear? Of women appearing in public in shorter than ankle-length skirts, or (gasp) a pair of pants? Three piece suits are no longer the absolute uniform of the work world replaced instead with more casual and comfortable attire. Similarly, language has become more relaxed, and in a great many instances, downright sloppy. We must be careful that our language skills, or lack thereof, do not create opportunities to be deemed less intelligent than is our due. To use a bit of hyperbole here, each time an individual uses "like," "literally," or "yup," rather than correct terminology, their IQ seems to be reduced by 10 points. This is hardly the way to make friends and influence people.

CHAPTER 2

Understanding
Generational Differences

As we look ahead into the next century,
leaders will be those who empower others.

~Bill Gates

A sk any leader of business and they will tell you there has been a massive change in the expectations of their position. Gone is the dictatorship regime of command and control. Gone is the mentality of superiority. Gone is the fear of the boss. What has replaced them is very different:

- Teamwork, collaboration, and cooperation are the key to success.

- Leaders must not set themselves apart from their teams.

- Mutual trust and respect is vital.

- Clear and respectful communication between all parties must be clear, continual, and open.

- All individuals must feel appreciated, seen, heard, and celebrated.

According to Loretta Cella, leaders have influence over much more than mere business. Leaders assist people to understand their deep value in the world and take inspired action to become more global citizens. Ms. Cella believes that leaders:

- are unafraid to step out of their "box"

- are unafraid to declare their mission

- actively engage in critical thinking

- enjoy open and frank conversations

- understand the value of systems, personal and business foundations

- word diligently to cultivate their authentic self

- understand the embrace the value of local, national, and global community

- believe in the tenants of service, and

- believe in the power of passion

Having now added some fodder to the vat of information about leadership responsibilities, perhaps it is appropriate that we reconsider the four statements made at the beginning of the first chapter pertaining to business leadership.

The theory for exploration included, that leaders should:

- Focus on relationships not facts.
- Add value by enabling things to happen, not by doing the work.
- Practice seeing the bigger picture, not mastering the details.
- Rely on "executive presence" to project confidence, not on having all the facts or answers.

Have your thoughts on these statements changed?

In the 21st century, business leadership is no longer defined as a corner office with a door. It is no longer enough to understand profit and loss, marketing and selling, and business to business association. Softer skills such as people skills, communication skills, and delegation skills have become hugely important. Why the change? What has happened to cause such an about-face to the expectations of leaders in business?

The answer lies in the change of the attitudes and expectations of the workforce, and those attributes are very, very different indeed.

It's an interesting time to be a business leader. It wouldn't be at all outrageous to see 4 generations of people working under the same roof, and being led by a single vision. We've got the:

Baby boomers (1945-1960),
Generation x (1960 – 1980),
Generation Y, the Millenniums (1980-2000), and
Generation Z, the up and comers (2000 -),

….all of whom are motivated by completed different ideals.

We've got the nose to the grind stone post-war generation, the skeptical and ever suspicious Generation X folk, the, "I turned up so I deserve the cream," Millennials, and the fearless and analytical Generation Z group.

Modern business demands that leaders understand how to motivate, how to lead through involvement, and how to encourage and reward innovative thinking.

Business leaders of the 21st century understand that each of the generations in today's workforce are motivated by different values, they must know how to tap into the strengths of each of the groups, they must address their responsibility to mentor and create new leaders, and they must bridge the gaps between the generations so the entire group can work together as a successful, cohesive unit.

Wow. No pressure there.

Let us first define and clarify the generations.

The first wave of Baby Boomers were born between the years of 1946-1954 into a world of promise. For them, work was an exciting adventure in a brave new and free world. Most have already entered retirement, but some are still living their business dream and are having a great time doing it. These individuals needed to hear that they were important to the success of the business.

The second wave of Baby Boomers, (1955-1965) are verging on retirement. For them, work was still an adventure, but it became a little more arduous. They became a little bit disillusioned with the business leaders of the day and didn't really trust them to have the individual's best interests at heart. Baby Boomers II need to hear that they matter.

Generation X people were born between 1963 and 1980. These were the latch-key kids, survivors, skeptical, and self-reliant. A large part of today's workforce, these individuals are self-starting free agents, they enjoy technology, and tend to be suspicious of others' motivations. They tend to view work as a necessary challenge. These individuals want to hear that leaders value their ideas.

On to Generation Y, known as the Millennials...the much-maligned masses. This group has turned the work world on its head. For them, work is a meaningful means to an end. They ask, "Why?" about everything causing infinite frustration to the reigning authority. They need to be respected by their leaders, crave instant gratification, and want to know that they and their co-workers can, "turn this place around."

Generation Z is just beginning to enter the workforce. They are eager to participate, and have little patience for repetition. They were born into the world of technology and wield it brilliantly. This group sees work as a means to a better world; they tend to view things from a global perspective. They want to know that the world needs them.

Savvy employers are aware that Generation X prefers carefully funneled information; Generation Y feeds on mentorship and praise, and the upcoming Generation Z are demanding respect for their technological prowess and their big-picture mentality. They also realize that the Baby Boomers (and to a lesser degree, Generation X) and the Millennials butt heads at every turn. To strengthen multi-generational relationships, leaders need to understand the needs, values, and motivational forces that speak to each of the groups.

IN PRAISE OF GENERATION X, Y, and Z:
Understanding the Great Divide

The past version of decision-making and leadership, rightly or wrongly, is being threatened, and leaders and managers are reeling primarily because the workforce will no longer abide the tenets of the hierarchical business structure. We are smack dab in the middle of a massive upheaval in societal and business norms and being successful requires that we respect the systems of the past, retain that which still has value, and adapt to the new expectations.

Being a business owner, employer or leader in today's business world requires an awareness of the needs of Baby Boomers, Generations X, Y, and Z. We interact with people of all ages in our business, personal and social lives. Whether engaging with staff, clients, or your children, understanding the differences in values and what motivates each individual will help make you a better communicator, employer, parent, and business owner.

Change has always been inevitable and is occurring faster than ever before.

Once upon a time, humans lived in caves and communicated through body language and the occasional grunt. The discovery of fire caused massive change, as did the invention of language. We changed from searching for food to cultivating it. The ripples of change resulting from the invention of the printing press quickly turned into a tsunami of written communication. It wasn't so very long ago that women were finally deemed to be people and not mere possessions; consider the upheaval created when women struggled for the right to vote!

Some generations have caused more of a ruckus than others; at this moment, it's the Millennial Generation, Generation Y that has been getting a lot of bad press. Entitled, self-absorbed, and unfocused are typical adjectives swimming in the ocean of negativity describing our majority generation in today's workforce. They cannot survive without their cell phones, have grown up playing video games, and expect instant gratification. They can't make a decision without consulting everyone they know, are generally lazy, and expect respect just for showing up.

Does all this sound familiar? It should, because similarly harsh criticisms of each new generation have rung through the rafters time after time after time. Think back to the panicked parents of teenagers when Chubby Checkers became popular. Remember the "rebels" created by The Beatles? What about the sacrilegious burning of draft cards? Think back through history. Young upstarts have created chaos with every passing generation, and for that we should be absolutely grateful!

Without new and innovative ideas, nothing changes, and without change we first stagnate and then fall into ruin. Do you really think Benjamin Franklin's parents thought him brilliant for playing with a kite in a rain storm? Did Thomas Edison's peers cheer him on to create the first light bulb, or did they quietly snicker behind his back? Can you imagine what Bell's family thought of their son wasting time by dreaming up a contraption for talking to someone out of ear shot?

Is there really anything different about this generation's progress than has come before?

Yes, and yes again.

While our Generation Y group may well be entitled and demanding, and even arrogant, let us remember, they were raised to be special. We bought them trophies even when they lost, and we rewarded them for anything and everything they undertook. Through buying them electronics, we taught them to understand the world of quick responses, and have instant information at their fingertips. They took advantage of every opportunity to learn the complex world of computers, and we praised them for their ingenuity to solve problems in a flash. We provided cell phones so we could keep in touch with them, and they took advantage of that technology to keep in touch with the world and with each other.

Noted speaker and author, Dov Baron calls this group, "Baby Boomers with balls." Just as with the Baby Boomers and their radical opinions (for the time), Gen Y's wants to change the world. Unlike the Boomers who only had access to pickets and sit in's to make themselves heard, this generation has the World Wide Web as their far more powerful and effective vehicle, and they are not afraid to use it!

Never before has a generation made such advances in such a short time, but every generation has changed the ways of the world: Baby Boomers turned most of the world on its ear, Generation X caused huge disruption, Generation Y even more so, and now enter from stage left, Generation Z.

If ever there was a group more poised, ready, and capable of making great advances, and massive improvements to our planet, I don't know which it might be. Where previous generations were fearful of change and determined to hold onto the status quo, Generation Z views it as exciting and normal.

Generation Z have never known a world without cell phones, computers, and multiple personal devices. Generation Z are being raised amid institutional and economic instability, informed by the looming shadow of depleting resources and planetary warming, and are globally connected via social media. They have always had information at their fingertips, and are masters at analytics.

Using the same leadership techniques with all the individuals of all these generations and expecting the same results from each simply cannot work. It is time for leaders to recognize that what got them here, will not get them further, and that what worked in the past may have outlived its usefulness. It is not the individuals in the workforce that are going to change; they feel completely justified to act and think as they do, so it falls to the leaders to become the catalysts for creating workplace environments in which individuals can perform well and provide companies with the greatest value for their wage dollars.

GENERATION SYNOPSES

The key to successful leadership today is influence,
not authority.

~ Kenneth Blanchard

Leaders have always known that to truly understand a situation is to be able to control that situation. To truly understand what drives the actions of people is to be able to motivate, inspire, and influence them.

To a degree, we are all products of our environment; we are heavily influenced by the prevailing values in our homes, our communities, our places of work, and across the globe. It is impossible to uncover fundamental reasons for behaviors and attitudes without an examination of major events in history. To that end, the information that follows, while not intended to be complete in any sense, is an abbreviated history of world events that helped to shape the general attitudes and characteristics of the North American population.

(Please note that the years of birth are approximate, there is no line in the sand, and no abrupt changes of behavior from one generation to the next.)

The Depression Era 1930-1945

Silent Generation, Traditionalists, Swing Generation

World Events

- *1929 stock market crash precipitates global depression.*
- *1929 England's Privy Council rules that women are, "persons;" in 1930, Cairine Wilson becomes Canada's first woman senator.*
- *Nazi's begin rise to power, Hitler becomes fuehrer. World War II begins and ends and includes the Holocaust.*
- *USSR recognized by U.S.*
- *Amelia Earhart is first woman to fly Atlantic solo.*
- *Prohibition repealed.*
- *Einstein writes about feasibility of atomic bomb.*
- *NBC begins first official television network.*
- *Income tax withholding introduced.*
- *Declaration of United Nations signed.*
- *Dionne sisters, first quintuplets to survive infancy, born in Canada.*
- *Roosevelt opens stage 2 of New Deal in USA calling for social security, better housing, equitable taxation, and farm assistance.*
- *Spanish civil war begins.*
- *Wrong-Way Corrigan flies from New York to Dublin.*
- *Fair Labor Standards Act establishes minimum wage.*
- *Orson Welle's broadcasts "War of the Worlds."*
- *More than 200,000 Japanese living in Canada and western USA moved to "relocation centers."*

- *Mussolini deposed.*
- *International Monetary Fund and World Band created.*
- *Woody Guthrie records, "This Land is Your Land."*
- *Trans-Canada Airlines (later Air Canada) makes the first scheduled passenger flight from Vancouver to Montreal.*
- *Unemployment Insurance Commission is introduced in Canada.*
- *Germany surrenders, Hitler commits suicide.*
- *USA drops atomic bombs on Hiroshima and Nagasaki.*
- *First electronic computer, ENIAC, built.*
- *First Canadian nuclear reactor goes into operation.*
- *Canadian family allowance payments begin for children under 16 and attending school.*
- *Canada's largest on-land earthquake shakes Central Vancouver Island (7.3 on the Richter scale). Felt from Oregon to Alaska and east to the Rocky Mountains.*
- *Prospectors strike oil in Leduc, Alberta, beginning Alberta's oil boom.*
- *Canada's biggest earthquake (8.1 on Richter scale) in the 20th century hits Queen Charlotte Islands in British Columbia. Felt over much of western North America.*
- *The construction of the 7,821km Trans-Canada Highway starts; designed to link the Atlantic and Pacific Oceans.*
- *Heart pacemaker invented in Canada by Winnipeg native John Hops.*
- *Foot and Mouth Disease in Saskatchewan results in the slaughter of thousands of animals setting the stage for the world recognized,*

rigorous Canadian regulations regarding the health of domestic livestock.

Generational Characteristics

- 1929 Stock Market Crash ushered in the Great Depression, followed by the time of global war, with the atomic bomb ushering in the age of nuclear threat.

- Patriotic, accepted a sense of deferment, and felt responsible to leave a legacy for their children.

- War, the threat of nuclear war, germ warfare, and other such fears meant that this generation was always uncomfortable and uncertain. They valued security, social tranquility, conformity, and togetherness. They responded to authority, celebrities, and institutions. They prefer formal language, formal salutations, firm handshakes, upright posture, and direct eye contact.

- Tend to be conservative, compulsive savers, maintain low debt, and use more secure financial products like Canada Savings Bonds versus stock market investments.

- Tend to feel a responsibility to leave a legacy to their children.

- Tend to be patriotic, oriented toward work before pleasure, respect for authority, and a sense of moral obligation.

- Tend to share a common goal of defeating the Axis powers.

- Accept sense of "deferment," contrasted with the emphasis on "me" in the Gen X group.

- Enjoyed significant opportunities in jobs and education as the War ended, and a post-war economic boom struck America.

- Due to growth of Cold War tensions, the potential for nuclear war and other never before seen threats, levels of discomfort and uncertainty permeated the generation.

- Tend to value security, comfort, social tranquility, family togetherness, and conformity.

- Rely on tried, true, and tested ways of doing things, slow to embrace anything new, and distrusted change.

- Respond to authority, celebrities, and respected institutions.

- Desire high-quality goods

- Prefer formal written and face-to-face language, formal salutations such as Sir or Madam, a firm handshake, upright posture, and direct eye contact.

Boomers I 1946-1954

Baby Boomers, Me Generation

World Events

- *World-wide war recovery efforts.*
- *Churchill', "Iron Curtain" speech marks beginning of Cold War.*
- *Soviet Union rejects American plan for UN atomic-energy control.*
- *Chuck Yeager breaks the sound barrier.*
- *Newfoundland joins Canada*
- *Gandhi assassinated.*
- *Eisenhower becomes president of U.S.A.*
- *Government officials indicted and executed as spies.*
- *Racial segregation in military ends.*
- *Nation of Israel proclaimed.*

- *Unrest in Middle East*
- *Republic of Korea proclaimed, Korean War begins and ends.*
- *Rock and Roll music becomes popular.*
- *European Economic Community (EEC) established.*
- *West Germany established.*
- *East Germany established under Soviet rule, followed by being granted sovereignty*
- *Communist People's Republic of China proclaimed by Mao Zedong.*
- *Egypt becomes republic.*
- *NATO treaty signed by 12 nations.*
- *First successful soviet atomic test.*
- *South Africa institutionalizes apartheid.*
- *Hydrogen bomb development begins in USA.*
- *Color television introduced to the U.A.*
- *George VI dies; daughter becomes Elizabeth II*
- *Watson & Crick discover signature of DNA.*
- *Hillary and Norgay reach summit of Mt. Everest.*
- *First atomic submarine Nautilus launched.*
- *U.S. Supreme Court unanimously bans racial segregation in public schools.*
- *8 nations sign Southeast Asia Defense Treaty (SEATO).*
- *End of first Indochina War – Vietnam partitioned.*
- *Salk begins inoculating children against polio.*
- *Gandhi's civil disobedience movement leads to an independent India.*

Generational Characteristics

- Bounded by the Kennedy and Martin Luther King assassinations, the Civil Rights Movement, and the Vietnam War (in which they either fought or protested).

- World-wide war recovery efforts, technological advances, and pushing limits brought good economic opportunities.

- They were indulged as youth in an era of community spirited progress, and they define themselves by their career, lifestyles, and attitudes. Many are workaholics.

- Had good economic opportunities and were largely optimistic about the potential for their countries and their own lives (the Vietnam War, notwithstanding).

- Value individualization, self-expression.

- Prestige conscious and enjoy public recognition

- Other resources cite this summary of the characteristics of the Boomers:

Equality, freedom, civil rights, environmental concern, peace, optimism, challenge to authority, protest. Baby Boomers mostly lived safe from war and serious hardship; grew up mostly in families, and enjoyed economic prosperity more often than not. Teenage/young adulthood years 1960-1980 - fashion and music: fun, happy, cheery, sexy, colorful, and lively.

Boomers II 1955-1965

Generation Jones, Love, Woodstock, or Sandwich Generation

World Events

- *Churchill resigns.*
- *West Germany becomes sovereign state.*
- *Rosa Parks refuses to sit at the back of the bus.*
- *Martin Luther King Jr. leads black boycott of Montgomery, Ala. Bus system leading to desegregated service.*
- *Nikita Khrushchev denounces Stalinism.*
- *First aerial H-bomb tested – 10 million tons TNT equivalent.*
- *Workers and students rebel against Communism in Hungary and Poland.*
- *St. Lawrence Seaway in Canada officially opens*
- *Suez Canal comes under siege.*
- *Canada's Lester Pearson wins the Nobel Prize for proposing a United Nations peacekeeping force to prevent war over control of the Suez Canal.*
- *Morocco gains independence.*
- *Unrest in USA regarding full integration in schools.*
- *Russians launch sputnik I. Space age beings.*
- *Birth control pill approved as contraceptive.*
- *America and Russia continue spy-related disputes.*
- *Communist China and Soviet Union split in conflict over Communist ideology.*
- *Dalai Lama flees Tibet from Chinese persecution.*

- *Senegal, Ghana, Nigeria, Madagascar, and Zaire (Belgian Congo) gain independence.*

- *Tensions begin to build between Cuba and the USA leading to Cuban Missile Crisis in 1962.*

- *John F. Kennedy inaugurated as president of USA. Later assassinated in 1963*

- *Moscow announces Gagarin as first man in orbit around Earth.*

- *USA spaceman, Sheppard, Grissom, Glenn and Soviet Titov explore space around Earth.*

- *Berlin Wall erected.*

- *USSR fires 50 megaton hydrogen bomb, the biggest explosion in history.*

- *The last weld is completed on the TransCanada Pipeline.*

- *Queen Elizabeth II and U.S. President Dwight Eisenhower officially open the St. Lawrence Seaway, which lets ocean vessels reach the Great Lakes.*

- *Canadian Native Indians get right to vote in Canadian elections.*

- *Canada's biggest meteorite fall in Bruderheim, Alberta; more than 300kg recovered from field.*

- *The FLQ explodes bomb in Montreal, Canada.*

- *Canadian Marshall McLuhan publishes Understanding the Media helping the world understand the changes technology was bringing to the world.*

- *Canada becomes third nation in space with the launch of satellite Alouette I.*

- *First artificial heart implant attempted.*

- *Martin Luther King Jr. delivers, "I have a dream," speech.*

- *Washington to Moscow 'Hot line" communications link opens to reduce risk of accidental war.*

- *Kenya receives independence.*

- *Nelson Mandela sentenced to life imprisonment.*

- *The Beatles appear on The Ed Sullivan Show.*

- *Malcolm X, black-nationalist leader, shot to death.*

- *Demonstrations and riots in USA as Blacks continue to fight for equality.*

- *USA troops land in Dominican Republic as fighting persists between rebels and Dominican army.*

- *Beginning of 20-year war in Vietnam*

- *Unrest in Middle East ongoing*

Generational Characteristics

Where Boomers I had the Cold War and Vietnam War, Boomers II had space exploration, heart transplants and AIDS.

- Humans landed on the moon. The personal computer and mobile phones came into existence.

- Government failures such as Watergate led to decreasing trust in authority, a dislike of bureaucracy, and loyalty to their own causes.

- More price conscious than Boomer I, value service and simple facts upon which to make decisions.

- Economic strugglers arose from larger Boomer I group having taken the best jobs, opportunities, housing, etc., affecting not only Boomers II, but Generation X as well.

- Increasingly environmentally conscious and as long as economical pricing is maintained supportive of "green" products and services.

- Missed the whole assassinations angst and Vietnam War turmoil.

- First post-Watergate generation losing much of its trust in government and optimistic view of Boomers I.

- Economic struggles rising from larger Boomer I group having taken the best jobs, opportunities, housing, etc. and in fact, affecting Gen X group as well.

- Suspicious of authority, self-centered.

- Dislike of bureaucracy but loyal to their chosen cause.

- Very aware of changing values, and of treating others as individuals.

- Personal gratification and public recognition highly valued.

Generation X 1965-1980

Baby Bust, Slackers, Why Me, or Latchkey Generation

World Events

- *Israel and Arab forces continue battling over Sinai Peninsula area including Suez Canal.*

- *Red China announces explosion of first hydrogen bomb.*

- *Cultural Revolution begins in China.*

- *Sir Francis Chichester first to sail around world single-handed.*

- *Che Guevara, Cuban revolutionary leader, killed in Bolivia.*

- *Racial violence continues in USA.*

- *Thurgood Marshall sworn in as first black Supreme Court justice.*

- *Christiaan N. Barnard and team of South African surgeons perform world's first successful human heart transplant.*

- *Dr. Martin Luther King Jr. slain*

- *Czechoslovakia invaded by Russians and Warsaw Pact forces.*

- *Stonewall riot in New York City marks beginning of gay rights movement.*

- *Armstrong, Aldrin Jr. and Collins take man's first walk on moon.*

- *1967 Flower Power at its height in California.*

- *Woodstock Festival.*

- *Sesame Street debuts.*

- *Internet (ARPA) goes online.*

- *Rhodesia declares itself a racially segregated republic.*

- *American troops invade Cambodia causing unrest in USA; anti-war militants attempt to disrupt government business in Washington. In 1973, American bombing of Cambodia ends marking official halt to 12 years of combat activity in Southeast Asia.*

- *Watergate scandal in USA leading to the impeachment and resignation of Richard Nixon*

- *Conflict in Middle East continues.*

- *1975, USA pulls out of Vietnam War.*

- *Apollo and Soyuz link-up in space.*

- *USA Supreme Court rules that blacks and other minorities are entitled to retroactive job seniority.*

- *USA Supreme Court rules that death penalty is a constitutionally acceptable form of punishment.*
- *First Female Episcopal priest ordained.*
- *Scientists identify bacteria causing Legionnaire's disease.*
- *Scientists report using bacteria in lab to make insulin.*
- *Nuclear-proliferation pact, curbing spread of nuclear weapons, signed by 15 countries including USA and USSR.*
- *Framework for Peace in Middle East signed by Egypt and Israel.*
- *Jim Jones' followers commit mass suicide in Jonestown, Guyana.*
- *Oil spills pollute waters in Atlantic and Gulf of Mexico.*
- *Canada Pension Plan created.*
- *Canada celebrates 100 years of Confederation (1967)*
- *Death penalty abolished in Canada*
- *Royal Commission on the Status of Women is appointed in Canada*
- *Breathalyzer is put into use in Canada.*
- *British Trade Commissioner James Cross kidnapped by the FLQ precipitating the War Measures Act allowing Canadians to be arrested and held without being charged.*
- *Quebec's Labor and Immigration minister, Pierre Laporte kidnapped and murdered.*
- *IMAX System developed in Canada.*
- *Rosemary Brown is first black woman elected to the provincial legislature in British Columbia.*
- *Canadian Paul Henderson scores in the eighth game of the Canada-Russia hockey series giving Canada a victory that may never be forgotten.*

- *Anik 1 Geo-stationary Commercial Satellite launched, making Canada the first country to use satellites for domestic communications.*

- *Canadian Blue Box Recycling Program launched playing a key role toward improving Canada's environment.*

- *Nuclear power plant accident at Three Mie Island, Pa.*

- *Iranian militants seize USA embassy in Tehran.*

- *Soviet invasion of Afghanistan stirs world protests.*

- *Continuing severe strife in the Middle East, Watergate, space exploration, Women's Rights, oil spills, and huge medical and technological advances.*

Generational Characteristics

Sometimes referred to as the "lost" generation, this was the first generation of "latchkey" kids, exposed to lots of daycare and divorce.

- Little faith in government, institutions or authority, lowest voting participation of any generation.

- Characterized by, "What's in it for me," attitudes, highly skeptical.

- Reaching adulthood during difficult economic times, success was not a given as it was for either of the Boomer generations.

- Far less traditional than predecessors, they took greater responsibility for raising themselves.

- Characteristics, lifestyles and attitudes center on balancing family life and work. They do not believe in sacrificing time, energy, and relationships for business advancement as did the Boomers.

- Pessimistic, disillusioned with almost everything, and very questioning of conventionality.

- Nothing is permanent. Multiculturalism and global thinking becomes more the norm. Waste reduction and recycling become important.

- Likely to be self-employed professionals embracing free agency over company loyalty.

- Lowest voting participation of any generation.

- Quoted by Newsweek as, "the generation that dropped out without ever tuning in to the social issues around them."

- Arguably the best educated generation with 29% obtaining a bachelor's degree or higher and therefore forming families with higher levels of caution and pragmatism.

- Valued family over company.

- Concerns run high over broken homes, kids growing up without a parent around, and over financial planning.

- Multiculturalism and global thinking becomes the norm.

- Require lots of stimuli, a challenging work environment, and flexibility without long-term commitment.

- Desire opportunities to learn, grow and improve.

- Like to be kept abreast of the large picture.

- Treat them like family but do not expect blind loyalty.

- The most price conscious of all the examined generations; they want to be paid well.

- Respond well to, "There aren't a lot of rules," and "Do it your way."

- Other resources cite the following characteristics of Generation X: Apathy, anarchy, reactionism, detachment, technophile, resentful, nomadic, struggling. Teenage/young adulthood years 1973-2000 - fashion and music: anarchic, bold, and anti-establishment.

Generation Y 1980-2000

Echo Boomers, Millennials, Why, We, iPod Generati

World Events

- *Indira Gandhi assassinated by Sikhs causing violence in India.*
- *USA breaks diplomatic ties with Iran as Middle East turmoil continues.*
- *Yugoslavia's six states begin to argue after Tito dies.*
- *Apartheid ends in South Africa. Nelson Mandela elected first black President.*
- *John Lennon of the Beatles shot and killed in New York City.*
- *President of Egypt, Anwar al-Sadat assassinated.*
- *Small Pox eradicated.*
- *Scientists identify AIDS as it becomes a major health threat.*
- *Mount St. Helens erupts in USA (1980) killing 60 people.*
- *Pac-Man video game released.*
- *Rubik's Cube becomes popular.*
- *Canadian hero, Terry Fox begins his "Marathon of Hope" run to raise money for cancer research.*
- *At least 1200 Canadians infected with AIDS and thousands more contracting Hepatitis C after receiving tainted blood transfusions.*

- *Canada gets new Constitution Act, including a Charter of Rights and Freedoms*
- *LAN developed in Canada allowing all computers in an office to communicate with each other.*
- *Canadarm, (Canadian Remote Manipulator System) takes first flight on space shuttle.*
- *Bertha Wilson is first Canadian woman appointed as Justice of the Supreme Court.*
- *Jeanne Sauve named Canada's first female Governor General. She was also the first woman Speaker of the House of Commons and the first female MP from Quebec to become a Cabinet Minister.*
- *Astronaut Marc Garneau, aboard the US space shuttle Challenger, becomes the first Canadian in space.*
- *Wheelchair athlete Rick Hansen leaves Vancouver on round-the-world "Man in Motion" tour to raise money for spinal-cord research and wheelchair spots.*
- *Lincoln Alexander becomes Ontario's first black Lieutenant Governor.*
- *John Polany of Toronto is co-winner of Nobel Prize for Chemistry.*
- *Canada receives United Nation award for sheltering world refugees.*
- *Tornado rips through Edmonton, killing 26 and injuring hundreds.*
- *Canada Supreme Court strikes down existing legislation against abortion as unconstitutional.*
- *Audrey McLaughlin becomes first woman to lead a federal political party in Canada.*
- *Fourteen female engineering students murdered by gunman at the University of Montreal.*

- *Heather Erxleben becomes Canada's first acknowledged female combat soldier.*

- *Land dispute causes 78-day armed confrontation between Mohawks and Canadian Army in Quebec*

- *Canadian Senate passes Goods and Services Tax.*

- *Canadian Wind Imaging Interferometer (WINDII) launches aboard NASA satellite to provide measurements of physical and chemical changes up to 300 kms above earth surface.*

- *David Schindler of the University of Alberta wins Stockholm Water Price for environmental research.*

- *Dr. Roberta Bondar becomes first Canadian woman in space, aboard US space shuttle, Discovery.*

- *Common-Law union recognized in Canada.*

- *Kim Campbell becomes Canada's first female Prime Minister.*

- *NAFTA (North American Free Trade Agreement) comes into effect.*

- *Canada's RADARSAT launched providing images of earth's surface, day and night, in any climatic conditions.*

- *13km bridge connecting Prince Edward Island to Canada's mainland opened.*

- *Canadian Donovan Bailey becomes "the world's fastest man" by breaking the record for the 100-metre race.*

- *Black Monday: worse market downturn in USA since the Great Depression*

- *World Wide Web invented.*

- *Hubble Telescope launched into space.*

- *Middle East crisis escalates leading to Operation Desert Storm.*

- *USSR dissolved signaling the end of the Cold War and the fall of Communism in Eastern Europe.*

- *Berlin wall demolished.*

- *Rwandan genocide of ethnic Tutsis by Hutus.*

- *Coloreds and Asians allowed to vote in South Africa.*

- *Chunnel rail tunnel between England and France inaugurated.*

- *End of war in Bosnia, Herzegovina.*

- *Beginning and end of war in Chechnya.*

- *Hong Kong returns to Chinese rule.*

- *Exxon Valdez oil-spill in Alaska.*

- *US spacecraft begins exploration of Mars.*

- *North American Free Trade Agreement (NAFTA) established.*

- *Princess Diana killed in Paris car accident.*

- *Asian financial crisis.*

- *Mother Teresa dies after 50 years' work in India.*

- *Viagra licensed for use in USA.*

- *Euro launched on international currency markets*

- *Military coup led by Gen. Musharraf overthrows Pakistani government.*

- *China launches first spacecraft.*

- *Vladimir Putin becomes Russian President*

- *Quebec's Parti Quebecois voted out of power in Canada. Referendum to secede from Canada dropped.*

Summary of Generation Y World Events

- *AIDS becomes a major health threat, Small Pox is eradicated; Terry Fox and Rick Hansen raise money for medical research.*

- *Indira Gandhi, Anwar Sadat assassinated, John Lennon assassinated*

- *Apartheid ends in South Africa, fourteen female students murdered at University of Montreal, legislation against abortion in Canada struck down.*

- *Women enter traditionally male roles in the armed forces, politics.*

- *GST in Canada*

- *Pac-Man released, World Wide Web invented, Hubble Telescope launched into space.*

- *Google, Facebook, social everything becomes the norm*

- *Berlin wall demolished, USSR dissolved, and Middle East Crisis leads to Operation Desert Storm.*

- *Exploration of Mars begun.*

- *Mind-boggling technological advances.*

Generational Characteristics

This generation is the children of the original Baby Boomers and is the cause of multiple treatises and books such as, <u>Now I Know Why Tigers Eat their Young</u>, and parental controls on televisions, telephones, and computers.

- This was the first generation to deal with the onslaught of massive amounts of information created by the invention of The Web. Teachers spent inordinate amounts of time persuading their students that just because it's on the internet doesn't mean that it's true.

- Global information created heighted social awareness and respect for ethnicities.

- They grew up in a time of immense and fast-paced change including full-time employment opportunities for women, dual-income families as the norm, and a wide variety of family types.

- They were more involved in family purchases from groceries to cars and many had credit cards co-signed by a parent. They are slow to progress to independence from parent influence.

- This was the beginning of the "Helicopter Parent," which continues to this day.

- They are swayed by organizations where missions speak to a greater purpose than the bottom line. They are shifting away from the materialism of the Boomers to search for inner tranquility and deeper meaning from life.

- They favor truth and authenticity.

- Honesty, humor, uniqueness, and information are important, and they value choice, customization, scrutiny, integrity, collaboration, speed, entertainment, and innovation.

- They are able to easily grasp new concepts and are very learning oriented. They are accustomed to a diverse universe where anything seems possible. Open-minded, optimistic, goal oriented, they are not as concerned with quality as variety, and they are very easily bored.

- They were born into a world where computers in homes and schools became the norm. Technological, electronic, and wireless society with global boundaries becoming transparent, have led them to be incredibly sophisticated technology-wise, immune to traditional marketing, but drawn to prestige purchases.

- They are incredibly self-absorbed, desire immediate gratification and with a desire for independence but lacking confidence to, "Fly without a net."

- Helicopter parenting and similar teacher attitudes have led to this group never being allowed to fail. Confidence doesn't come from success; it comes from surviving failure, so this group has substantially less confidence than previous generations. To counter their lack of self-assurance, they are image driven, with a greater need for peer acceptance, fitting in, and social networking.

- Millennials don't want bosses; they want coaches

- Feature the organization as an instrument of change, give them systematic feedback and allow them input into all things in which they participate.

- Able to easily grasp new concepts and are very learning oriented.

- Computers in homes and schools are the norm. Born into a technological, electronic, and wireless society with global boundaries becoming more transparent. They are accustomed to a diverse universe where anything seems possible.

- Much more racially and ethnically diverse and much more segmented as an audience (thanks to Cable TV channels, satellite radio, Internet, etc.)

- Incredibly sophisticated, technology wise, immune to traditional marketing but drawn to prestige purchases.

- Content is key and they strive to be creators, distributors, and users of content.

- Self-absorbed, with a desire for independence, but lacking confidence to "fly without a net."

- They want experience-based results and are not as concerned with the why of it.

- Image driven, with a greater need for peer acceptance, fitting in, and social networking.

- Open minded, optimistic, goal oriented, and successful through efficient multi-tasking. Easily bored. Are not as concerned with quality as variety.

- Honesty, humor, uniqueness, and information are important.

- They value choice, customization, scrutiny, integrity, collaboration, speed, entertainment, and innovation.

- Motivate them with sensory rich images and messages. Use language that paints visual pictures and action verbs that challenge.

- Send messages that stress team spirit: "You will be working with other bright, creative people," or, "You and your team can make this initiative a success."

- 9-5 work hours hold no interest for them. Allow flexible work schedules with this group.

- Key words are collaborate, connect, co-create, and control…mostly with their peers.

Generation Z 2000-

Tweens, Baby Bloomers, Generation 9/11

World Events

- *Anti-government militant sets off truck bomb explosion in Oklahoma.*

- *American President Clinton impeached, but Senate fails to get the 2/3 vote needed to carry out the order. Clinton remains in office, shaking the nation's confidence.*

- *1998, a hurricane rips across Central America killing an estimated 10,000 people.*

- *Most destructive ice storms in Canadian history (1998, 2013)*

- *The new Canadian Arctic territory of Nunavut is created.*

- *September 11, 2001, (9/11) attacks on World Trade Centers and Pentagon in USA leading to American invasion of Afghanistan and Iraq.*

- *Middle East war continues overthrowing government of Saddam Hussein.*

- *Osama bin Laden, believed to have ordered multiple terrorist attacks (including 9/11) killed by American forces.*

- *Boxing Day Tsunami (2004), caused by a 9.2 earthquake in the Indian Ocean resulted in 230,000 people killed in 14 different countries.*

- *Hurricane Katrina (2005) strikes Gulf Coast of USA leaving damage of over $100 billion.*

- *Launched on the 19th January 2006, Horizons sets out to study Pluto and its moons; expected to reach its destination by the 14th July 2015.*

- *2007 Burj Khalifa in United Arab Emirates becomes the world's tallest building at over 828 meters (2,716.5 feet) and 163 stories high.*

- *First American Black President, Barack Obama elected in 2008 and again in 2012.*

- *Cuba removed from Nations that Support Terrorism list.*

- *Myanmar (Burma) hit by Cyclone Nargis (2008) causing the death of 146,000 people.*

- *World financial collapse (2007-2009) worst financial collapse since the Great Depression resulting in global rise in unemployment levels. Countries and individuals still recovering in 2016.*

- *Haiti Earthquake (2010) results in the death of over 316,000 people.*

- *Tohoku Tsunami (2011) caused by a 9.0 earthquake off the coast of Japan led to the meltdown of the Fukushima Daiichi Nuclear Power Plant and causing the deal of 18,400 people.*

- *2011 Marijuana legalized in 2 US states.*

- *2013 Scientists successfully clone human stem cells from human skin cells, using the same technique that cloned molly the sheep.*

- *2014 - Facebook buys WhatsApp for an astonishing $19 Billion US Dollars.*

- *World oil price plunges to historical low*

- *European spacecraft Rosetta lands on comet.*

- *Bola virus outbreak*

- *Airplane carrying 298 people shot down over Ukraine.*

- *2015 - SpaceX lands rocket successfully & makes reuse possible.*

- *Climate change deal reached by about 200 countries*

- *Paris terrorist attack leaves hundreds dead.*

- *Russia intervenes in Syrian civil war.*
- *Flowing liquid water found on Mars.*
- *Iran nuclear deal reached.*
- *7.9 earthquake hits Nepal, kills over 8,000 people.*
- *2016 – Britain exits EU after referendum.*
- *World Top GO player defeated by Artificial Intelligence*
- *Zika Virus spreads across America*
- *North Korea claims successful H-bomb test.*
- *Middle East conflict continues.*

Generational Characteristics

- Smart phones, Apps, IPads, tablets, allows constant information flow across the globe, resulting in generational anxiety.

- Parents of this generation are likely older than in previous generations and are less likely to get divorced.

- This group faces an early graduation from childhood, entering the world of "teenage-hood" much sooner.

- They face global terrorism, the aftermath of 9/11, school violence, economic uncertainty, recession, and world-wide financial crises.

- These are the new conservatives embracing traditional beliefs, valuing the family unit, self-control, and responsibility. They value security more than ever before, and education is valued as a means of gaining it.

- They are growing up in the paranoid openness of the Information; they have been raised to keep safe and to be cautious of strangers.

- A higher level of educational technology and vast amounts of immediate information is leading to more emphasis on analysis and evaluation of data.

- Accustomed to high-tech and multiple information sources, with messages bombarding them from all sides. They have never lived without the Internet.

- They are the first generation to not need parents or teachers help them gather information from the Internet. Instant access to information has bolstered respect for knowledge.

- Instant access to information has shortened their attention span and heightened their awareness of visuals and other sensory input.

- They are impatient as they were raised in a world of technology and instant gratification.

- Data astute and computer savvy, this generation is frugal, has very little brand loyalty, and is much more focused on larger issues than any previous group.

- Peer acceptance is very important; they need to belong to not only their own group, but to the world as a whole.

- Globally diverse generation coming from a wider mix of backgrounds with different experience and ideas.

- They are ready to be on a mission, are confident, and very optimistic.

- They believe they can impact the world and can visualize changing places with someone and project possible behaviors.

- They are more imaginative than any other generation and more discerning, thinking carefully about all decisions.

- Interested in quality vs. quantity or variety.

- They place a high value on authenticity, and have a strong sense of right and wrong.

- They feel the world is a close-knit community and have taken global warming and care of the environment to heart.

- They know that being of service to others feels good.

- They will not abide leadership through intimidation or displays of physical power. They have information on their side, were raised in an atmosphere of, "It's cool to be smart," and know full well that they, "know more," than their bosses. Treat them as valued members of the team.

CHARACTERISTICS

For purposes of clarity and comparison, the charts that follow provide alternate means for viewing condensed versions of the characteristics, rationales, and simplification of some of the most major generational differences.

Generation X The Cowboys	Generation Y The Collaborators	Generation Z The Diversifiers
Conducting research required a trip to the library and the use of an index card file. Cell phones, if used at all, weighed about 2 lbs., were the size of a brick and held a whopping 30 minutes of talk time. Life was more linear, taking time to move from point A to B	Research involves opening multiple tabs in a browser while simultaneously playing Angry Birds. Constant communicators Life is circular and optimistic; like a Ferris wheel with lots of opportunity to stop, snap a picture, post it to Facebook, then continue on around the wheel.	Research involves customizing information Multiple mobile devices, constantly connected to the digital world Life is experience driven and paving new paths in the norm
Little supervision desired or expected **Influence through organization, position**	Heavily supervised team players and collaborators as children and expect teamwork as adults **Influence through networks, community**	Social media supervised Extremely visual and creative **Follow famous influencers to tap into aspirational lifestyles**

Generation X The Cowboys	Generation Y The Collaborators	Generation Z The Diversifiers
Learn one trade or area of expertise and stay in it. Racially similar Cautious Expect and expected to do one job and do it well. **Structure**	Continuous learners, highly educated Diverse, optimistic Achievement oriented Socially conscious **No structure; flexibility is highly valued**	Uninterested in mainstream Embrace diversity and desire to be first to find or create new trends. Personally connected to ultimate goals **Customized structure**
Job security	**Employability**	**Experiential**
Work = income	**Work = income & personal enrichment**	**Work = income, personal enrichment & personal connection**

RATIONALE

Generation X	Generation Y	Generation Z
Coaching	**Coaching**	**Coaching**
Command and control parents/employers. Slow movement through ranks expected. Individuals responsible for own engagement.	Raised with constant coaching and feedback and expect it in workplace. Will keep them engaged and can be as quick as an email, a text, or a 2-min. conversation	Will search for coaching on topics of interest. Will question & expect answers regarding rationale behind decisions. Will listen, add their own research, then make own conclusions.
Collaboration	**Collaboration**	**Collaboration**
Individual work as the norm. Clear boundaries understood. Deadlines were tight under threat of demotion, loss of promotion, job loss.	Natural collaborators especially when purpose and goals are understood. Deadlines and business boundaries should be made clear.	Multi-level collaborators. Not intimidated by titles. Set own ambitious deadlines. Boundaries will be pushed not out of disrespect but through creation of new ideas.
Measures	**Measures**	**Measures**
Report card style feedback. Fearful respect for authority and little input into measuring devices.	Raised with lots of structure and measuring systems; require understanding or how they will be judged and assessed.	Raised with flexibility and freedoms to choose. Candid conversations with clear expectations from both sides made clear.

Generation X	Generation Y	Generation Z
Motivation	**Motivation**	**Motivation**
Inner motivation and through fear of losing position or being overlooked for promotion. Work was required for income and was not designed for comfort.	Work environment should be comfortable and inspire them to contribute without fear of criticism. Benefit from instant rewards such as pizza lunch or time off for a job well done.	Environment is unimportant. Strive to find new answer, perspective, or system for problem solving. Will demand recognition for discoveries and follow-through.
Flexibility	**Flexibility**	**Flexibility**
Little opportunity to understand company as a whole. Occasional PD opportunities provided as budget allowed.	Provide with opportunities to learn and meaningfully contribute.	Expect to be able to contribute to the whole. Will not abide "keyhole approach." Provide with meaningful opportunities for proving their worth.
Leadership	**Leadership**	**Leadership**
Followed leaders perceived as fair and who gave any positive feedback. Leaders who offered mentorship were rare and highly valued.	Prefer to follow leaders who are honest, with integrity and who treat them with respect. Leaders should let them know the big pictures so they understand their roles.	Will not abide respect through fear authority. Will follow leaders who value ingenuity and diversity and allow them to be responsible for end results of their own ideas.

WORK EXPECTATIONS
Generational Workplace Differences I

Category	Boomers I	Boomers II	Gen X	Gen Y	Gen Z
Birth Year	1946–1954	1955–1965	1963–1980	1980–2000	1995–
Coming of Age	1967–1975	1976–1986	1984–2001	2001–2021	2008–
Meeting Style	Value meetings and opportunities to brainstorm	Value the invitation to participate, and eager to show themselves capable	Like meetings with a purpose; don't like to waste time; prefer independent time	Prefer short, casual meetings with team activities; want to be entertained	Eager to participate; little patience for repetition or delays
Attitude Toward Authority	Honor, respect	Disillusioned and untrusting	Skeptical, suspicious	Need to be respected by leaders	Need to be valued by leaders
Technology	Master it	Improve it	Enjoy it	Employ it	Adapt it
Interactive Style	Self-absorbed	Self-sufficient	Self-starting free agents	Team player	Collaborative
Work is...	An exciting adventure	An arduous adventure	A necessary challenge	Meant to be meaningful	A means to a better world
Characteristics	Driven, optimistic, competitive, think people should pay their dues	The "in-it-for-me" group, struggling to compete with Boomers I	Latch-key kids, survivors, skeptical, self-reliant	Ask why, prefers teamwork and supportive structure, craves feedback and instant gratification	Analytical information processors, world-wide collaborators, ready to tackle global issues
Message that Motivates	You are important to success	You matter	We need your ideas	You and your co-workers can turn this place around	The world needs you

Generational Workplace Differences II

Pre-1980	Post-1980
Working teams	Virtual Teams
Factory/office	Home/Mobile
Personal customer service	Call Centers
Line Management	Matrix Management
In-house services	Outsourcing and off-shoring
Job for life	Job for 2 years
Career for life	Career for 10 years
On-site services	On-line services
Few employee rights	Many employee rights
Low employee awareness	High employee awareness
Employee isolation	Employee connectivity
Reliable pensions	Unreliable pensions
Other: inequality, discrimination, minimal training, telephone, letters, mainframe computers, sub-contracting, employment contracts	Other: work/life balance, sabbaticals, life- long learning, employee ownership, social enterprise, email, social networking, mobile web, globalization, psychological contracts

Gen X Tip

You must earn their loyalty with each and every meeting. It's a challenge to keep them. Why? Because Gen X is unforgiving when disappointed. They won't give you a second chance.

Gen Y Tip

Gen Y's come from a world where everything changes all the time and seldom with warning. To keep them engaged, offer them diversity of activities and embrace gamification. It's what they were raised on, after all.

Gen Z Tip

Gen Z's have never known a world without cell phones, computers, and multiple personal devices. They have always had information at their fingertips, are masters at analytics, and are poised to change the way the world does business.

MASLOW'S HIERARCHY OF NEEDS APPLIED TO EMPLOYEE ENGAGEMENT (Adapted)

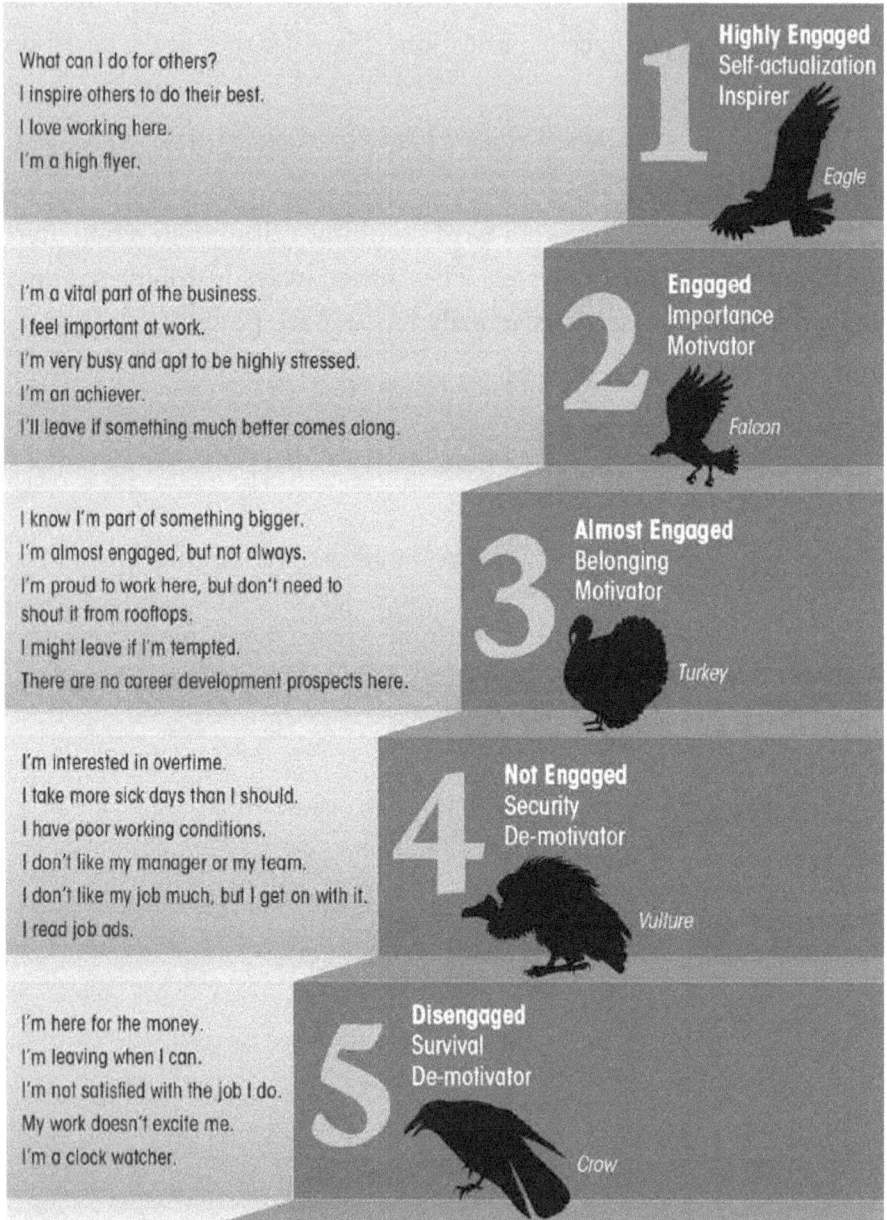

What can I do for others?
I inspire others to do their best.
I love working here.
I'm a high flyer.

Highly Engaged
Self-actualization
Inspirer

Eagle

I'm a vital part of the business.
I feel important at work.
I'm very busy and apt to be highly stressed.
I'm an achiever.
I'll leave if something much better comes along.

Engaged
Importance
Motivator

Falcon

I know I'm part of something bigger.
I'm almost engaged, but not always.
I'm proud to work here, but don't need to shout it from rooftops.
I might leave if I'm tempted.
There are no career development prospects here.

Almost Engaged
Belonging
Motivator

Turkey

I'm interested in overtime.
I take more sick days than I should.
I have poor working conditions.
I don't like my manager or my team.
I don't like my job much, but I get on with it.
I read job ads.

Not Engaged
Security
De-motivator

Vulture

I'm here for the money.
I'm leaving when I can.
I'm not satisfied with the job I do.
My work doesn't excite me.
I'm a clock watcher.

Disengaged
Survival
De-motivator

Crow

The chart that follows indicates the usual stages of Maslow's Hierarchy of Needs and at what stage of development these needs are ideally met.

Life Stage/Issues	Needs Stage
Infant – feeding, comfort, care	Biological and physiological care
Toddler – bodily functions, muscular control	Safety
Pre-school – exploration, discovery, play	Belonging, love
School child – achievement, accomplishment	Esteem
Adolescent – resolving identity with direction	Esteem
Young adult – intimate relationships, work, social life	Esteem
Mid adult – contribution	Self-actualization
Late adult – life meaning, life purpose, life achievements, contribution	Self-actualization

Because individuals are entering the workforce with less and less true life experience and requiring mentorship and guidance, it is reasonable to amend the ages suggested by Maslow to reflect today's stages of development. "Identity" is now sought far later than adolescence, and in fact, often changes with new opportunities and interests.

Today, "Achievement" is coveted far into the mid-adult range, as is intimacy, and social life. The need for "Belonging" is the most highly sought needs fulfillment category far into adulthood, and the category itself has expanded to include "Global Belonging."

Correlating the Needs and the Employee Engagement data results in the following:

Highly engaged	Eagle	Self-Actualization	Inspirer	Late Adult Mid Adult	Life purpose, contribution
Engaged	Falcon	Self-Actualization, Importance	Motivator	Mid Adult	Contribution
Almost Engaged	Turkey	Esteem, Belonging	Motivator	Young Adult	Intimacy, work, social life
Not Engaged	Vulture	Esteem, Security	De-motivator	Adolescent	Identity
Disengaged	Crow	Esteem, Survival	De-motivator	School age	Achievement
				Pre-school	Belonging
				Toddler	Safety
				Infant	Basic care

In essence, what we are witnessing is needs fulfillment being required well beyond previously expected ages, and now being asked of not only parents and teachers, but from leaders in the workplace as well. Whether we like it or not, if we are to be great leaders and thereby inspire others to greatness, Needs Fulfillment for our workforce must be moved up the priority list.

Eliezer Yudkowsky, author of Harry Potter and the Methods of Rationality, says;

"Not every change in an improvement but every improvement is a change; you can't do anything better unless you can manage to do it differently. It's time to do coaching differently. It's time to treat it like the transferable skill that it is. Now more than ever, we're in a time of change and uncertainty. By increasing your coaching skills, you increase the chances of seeing positive change for you, for your organization and for the next generation of leaders."

THE RISE OF WOMEN IN THE WORKFORCE

1976	2014
36% of women give birth to 4 or more children	12% of women gave birth to 4 or more children
22% of women gave birth to 2 children	35% of women gave birth to 2 children

Why the about-face in the birth data seen above? Reasons include the availability of the birth control pill, the growth of women's participation in the workforce, and the rising cost of raising children. During WW I and WW II, women proved they were capable of working jobs more typically assigned to men. At the same time, more women were entering and graduating from universities, and further, continuing to enter post graduate programs, resulting in the age at first marriage rising significantly. The right to socially accepted birth control, including abortion, allowed women more control over their situations, ultimately resulting in many more women in powerful business leadership roles.

Where previously male decision-makers were predominantly left-brain driven, logical, and linear, predominantly right-brained female leaders now added new ingredients and perceptions into the mix. The rise in the power of women's rights changed the status quo not only in business, politics, and the military, but in the home.

Where traditionally it was the fathers wielding ultimate power and "final say," women were no longer satisfied to accept the submissive role, thus challenging preconceived ideals of proper child rearing. Where once it was considered a weakness for a boy to cry, for example, more vocal maternal influences have amended that attitude to young men as, "being in touch with their feelings." Young men previously preened into become the, "man of the house" and following in their fathers' footsteps as quickly as possible, now were encouraged to explore their options and choose a path that would see to their emotional happiness.

With women having fewer children, and by virtue of genetic maternal instincts, each child began to take on special significance. What with working 40 hours and more each week, mothers tended to be somewhat loathe to let a moment of their offspring's precious childhood slip by and subconsciously strove to make up for lost time by encouraging their children to remain "young" as long as possible. Since the wives and mothers were working full time, household chores started to become more fairly split between the spouses and without the more natural ease of the maternal instinct to guide them internally, the men followed the examples the women set. The stage for our entitled younger generations became more solidified.

Divorce also became more prevalent, with children custody, more often than not, being awarded to the mothers, and the female influence becoming even stronger.

Let's add the changes in the attitudes of educators to the equation. Budget constraints and hierarchies demand that schools be run as businesses with projected population numbers being the basis for government-allotted monies. Schools must attract the best teachers to ensure board satisfaction, and increasingly, student success. School trustees and principals, until quite recently were predominantly male. Discipline was strict and corporal punishment the norm. Children sat in rows, did their work individually and silently, libraries were filled with books and conversations about the reading materials was not encouraged. Teachers and principals were the authorities and parents echoed that understanding at home. Schools maintained an untouchable hierarchy with the principals having to walk the line between satisfying the responsibilities of both leader and manager. Where once "strapping" students was punishment, pure and simple, the softer appeal of "behavior modifying incentives" became more prevalent and the primarily female teachers were quick to adopt the new attitude. Students were permitted to bring more individuality to their assignments, and guiding them to find that individuality gathered popularity. Soon enough, the role of teacher began to morph from the lecturer at the front of the room to something quite different. Teachers became more like, "learning facilitators," and student rights became all important.

Can it be only coincidence that education has become more child and individual-centric as women have accepted decision-making roles in education? Doubtful.

With gender responsibilities no longer being as clear as in years past, the role of family "head" in now more commonly split among available talent. Just as they are receiving at home and in schools, Generation Y and Z are demanding the same individual attention and emotional care in the work world. They want to be nurtured and guided, and that is one of the strengths of the right-brained.

Given the needs of the current workforce, it seems that the inherent strengths of women might be in high demand. In business, leadership roles are still sought and achieved by more men than women, but it won't be too much longer before gender equalization sees a more equitable balance. It will be interesting to see if that, in and of itself, has an influence on the gap between the generations in business.

THE DOPAMINE EFFECT
AND THE RISE OF THE HELICOPTER PARENT

Simon Sinek posted an article about on Facebook early in 2017 about the dopamine effect that got a lot of attention, and rightfully so. The reference to the addictive nature of the dopamine response is particularly interesting not only because of its effects on Gen Y, but, in my opinion, to the entire population.

Imagine that you are living in an age where birth control is readily available to the masses and you now have control over family planning. You have delayed that first baby until the time is right. Food, shelter, and clothing are no longer the prime considerations, and the "hormone-o-meter" is screaming for procreation. Finally, unto you a child is born, cute as a bug's ear, and undeniably bound for greatness.

You have researched parenting techniques, a safety-conscious crib, a pacifier that will not harm tooth development, and toys that promise to supply appropriate stimulation and learning opportunities. You know how and what to feed your innocent babe, and what to expect at every stage of development.

In comes the dopamine effect.

The very first time you pop that special pacifier into your child's mouth and hear the suckling sounds as he or she accepts the comfort you have provided, you feel a flash of satisfaction that all your research and effort have paid off. You are a good parent! Your child is content and you have aided in that contentment.

As baby grows, you continue to do your utmost to provide the best possible opportunities for the child's success. Each time your efforts are rewarded by him or her reaching a new milestone of development, another dose of dopamine is administered, and you take some credit for the child's accomplishment.

One of your jobs as a new parent is to protect your infant from harm; this is natural and normal as human babies cannot survive without parental aid. Each time we "save" our child from a boo-boo, ta da! We are rewarded with another shot of "feel good" juice. Every gift we present to them, every hug of thanks we receive from them, feeds our understanding that they love us, and that we are good parents. We become so addicted to this euphoria of dopamine, that we actively cultivate opportunities for the child to bestow their smiles upon us. Additionally, because we have provided the best equipment and the best environments for their learning, we celebrate their milestones with them, as if they were our own.

Our child is special and we take extraordinary pains to ensure that he or she lives every moment with that knowledge. We heap praise upon them for every little thing and ask nothing in return but a smile. And why not? That smile supplies us with our "fix" of confidence in our ability as parents. When the inevitable day arrives when we are not rewarded with a smile or any gratitude at all, it certainly is not the child at fault; it must absolutely be the result of us not satisfying their needs sufficiently well and so we up the ante and provide more opportunities for them to offer us a reward.

Add to this scenario the public opinion poll of what a good parent is. The ruthless competition between parents to be the poster person of excellent parenting is exactly that: ruthless. Good parents pack only the most gourmet of lunches. Good parents walk or drive their children to and from school. Good parents leave their jobs and other responsibilities to act as a courier service for items their children have forgotten at home. Good parents provide name-brand clothing, and the latest and greatest electronics and games. Good parents are not good parents if their child must face consequences for their mistakes because truly good parents would not have allowed their child to make a mistake in the first place.

The irony is that without mistakes from which to learn and recover, these oh-so-special and over-loved children do not receive the opportunity to prove themselves to themselves, thereby remaining dependent on their parents and woefully lacking in self-confidence.

So many well-intentioned parents go to the ends of the earth to ensure their child always feels loved, pampered, and special, in no small part to ensure their dopamine is delivered on time and in abundance. The education systems, too, are victims of the need to have their students succeed. The reasons are different, but the results are the same. Schools are far more child-centered than they have ever been, and there are many very excellent reasons for it. Even so, I stand firm in my conviction that the feeling that we are the reason behind our children's successes is a driving force behind many of the behaviors we are currently witnessing, with good intentions being the motivator, and the feel-good effects of dopamine being the ultimate prize.

Now we have both parents and young people addicted to having their needs met through regular infusions of dopamine, and weaning off the drug is difficult. For leaders in the business world, more and more, it is falling to them to direct, coach, and mentor the newest recruits to the workforce back to reality and the less fuzzy and friendly world of work.

GENERATIONAL NEEDS

Needs of Generation Y

A recent article on social media featured the author's views view on Millennials at work, what they wanted, and what leaders ought to do to meet their needs. A brief synopsis of the highlights of that article follows:

- It is crucial for this generation to understand not only what is expected of them, but what it means to the corporation as well.

- They believe they are over-qualified for entry-level jobs.

- They want to make a difference on day one. Give them some responsibility, and more importantly, give them feedback. Don't criticize; they don't handle that well.

- Millennials are likely to change jobs 3 or 4 times before they land somewhere they want to stay.

- Just because their requests seem outrageous to you, it doesn't make them wrong.

- You must be honest and upfront with this generation; they have the world at their fingertips and will know if they are being manipulated or conned.

- Millennials are smart, hardworking, socially conscious, and want to make a difference in your organization. You just need to let them. Teach them what they need to know, provide a lot of feedback, and show them a path to success. If all else fails, call their parents. Did I happen to mention they are the most connected generation to their parents? Millennials rely on their parents for advice and direction.

2016 Gallup Chairman and CEO, Jim Clifton offered his opinion as follows:

- Millennials don't just work for a paycheck – they want a purpose. They want to work for organizations with a mission and purpose.

- Millennials are not pursuing job satisfaction - they are pursuing development. Giving out toys and entitlements is a mistake and it's condescending. Purpose and development drive this generation.

- Millennials don't want bosses – they want coaches. They want to be valued as people and employees, and they want to be coached to understand and build their strengths.

- Millennials don't want annual reviews – they want ongoing conversations. Millennial conversations are in real time and continuous; yearly reviews don't qualify.

- Millennials don't want to fix their weaknesses – they want to develop their strengths. Weaknesses never develop into strengths while strengths develop infinitely. Weaknesses should not be ignored, but they should be minimized while strengths are maximized.

- It's not my job – it's my life. Does this organization value my strengths, my contributions, and offer me the opportunity to do what I do best every day?

- Millennials don't just work for a paycheck – they want a purpose, meaningful work. Compensation must be fair but is no longer the driver. Emphasis has changed from $ for the Boomers to purpose for Gen Y

- Millennials are not pursuing job satisfaction – they are pursuing development. They don't care about the ping pong table in the break room and feel that toys and entitlements are condescending. Purpose and development drive this generation.

- Millennials don't want to have to balance work and life – they are prepared to make their work their life.

There you have it: the Generation Y wish list. How does that compare to the wish list of employers? What do business leaders want and expect from their employees, and since command and control is no longer acceptable, desirable, or functional, how do they get **their** needs met?

Needs of Generation X

Generation X, Y, and Z all have wish lists for the work place and because Generation Y has evolved over the cusp of the age of technology, their needs are louder and their list is lengthy. We must not forget, however, that Generation X would like their needs met as well. At this moment, Gen X are holding the majority of the leadership roles while Gen Y is causing the chaos, but that ratio will most certainly change as the need for superior technological understanding and ability continues to grow. (Considered in that light, it may well be that in the near future Gen Z will quickly eclipse Gen Y for the highest and most technologically demanding leadership positions. That will be an interesting transition.)

Since it falls to leaders to create environments where employees feel safe to think up new and better systems, products, and wonderful new ideas, and with Generation Y leading the technological knowledge race, it could well be that a Millennial will become the leader asking Generation X to follow their lead. What might that look like? A generational values and needs comparison might reveal some interesting information.

There are some very large gaps between the generational expectations of Gen X and Gen Y, but there are also a surprising number of similarities. One of the most major gaps results from hugely different parenting attitudes and techniques: the latchkey and independent children of Gen X vs. the over-protected children of Gen Y. Another is the willingness to rise up through the ranks of business: Gen X were willing to start in entry-level positions and were determined to prove their worth, while Gen Y believe their technological prowess should catapult them over bottom rung positions. Additionally, Gen X is accepting of hierarchical business structure, with top, middle, and lower positions, and a clear chain of command. Gen Y denies that system in favor of a circular structure embodying equality and collaborative teamwork across the company. Think, King Arthur and the Knights of the Round Table.

On the similarities side of the equation, both generations clearly question conventionality, place high value on family, and crave variety and challenge.

Generation X The Cowboys	Generation Y The Collaborators
Lost Generation, latchkey kids took greater responsibility for raising themselves	Helicopter parents always providing safety net for their children
Independence is highly valued and actively sought.	Value independence but lack the confidence to "fly without a net"
Skeptical, preponderance of "What's in it for me" attitude	Self-absorbed, and wanting instant gratification
Will perform duties as requested by leaders and bosses	Wanting to know reasons behind requests before complying.
Reached adulthood during difficult economic times	Little financial knowledge and responsibility resulting in poor money skills
Little value for loyalty	Peer loyalty is paramount
Cynical, pessimistic, questioning of conventionality	Accustomed to diversity, value transparency, choice has high value
Want to paid well; willing to work their way up through the ranks	Want to be paid fairly; believe they are "above" entry-level positions
Great concern over family vs. work	Family provides security for all things
Need flexibility and challenge at work	Easily bored, more concerned with variety than quality
Respond well to few rules and opportunity for individuality	Respond well to teamwork and collaboration

If a Gen Y individual was to lead a Gen X individual, where might difficulties arise? Would the collaborative, round-table leadership style of the Gen Y supply sufficient trust and confidence for Gen X or would it be read as wishy-washy, and incapable of making tough decisions?

Might the teamwork mentality, so desirable for Gen Y, lead to Gen X feeling smothered and stymied by the beloved but time-consuming democracy? The need for individuality and independence on the part of Gen X is one of its strongest characteristics; how will a Gen Y leader fulfill that all-important need for them amid a structure of teamwork and collaboration? An important factor in these two generations continually butting heads with each other involves the Law of Reciprocity (More on this in Chapter 3.)

The Law of Reciprocity says that when an individual receives a gift of perceived value, they immediately feel an urge to respond in kind. We see it all the time at birthdays and Christmas and other gift-giving celebrations, where the value of the gift given must match the value of the gift received. Even when no gift is expected in return, such as in the case in the birth of a baby, we still feel obliged to send a thank you card, even though we have thanked the giver profusely at the time of the giving. Additionally, we subconsciously look for ways to do a favor for them, or reciprocate in some other way until we feel the debt has been paid. Generation X and its predecessors felt the Law of Reciprocity very strongly; unfortunately, Generation Y and Z do not dance to the beat of that drum and it causes an enormous amount of animosity between the generations.

Gen X was raised to know that "please" was the Magic Word, and "Thank you" was the payment for something given. Even more, because of the lingering effects of the Great Depression, being in debt or indebted for anything, even a favor freely given, caused great anxiety and a driving need to be freed of its burden. Favors may well have been freely given, but there was an unstated accounting system that kept track of who did what for whom, and who still owed something in return. Even being invited to dinner absolutely had to be repaid in kind; if it was not, festering resentment began to build, and Gen X did not, as a rule, have forgiving natures. The indignity of not having a favor repaid could, given time, actually break a family apart.

Generation Y holds no such ownership of reciprocity. The urge to repay is not immediately kindled when presented with a gift or a kindness and the very notion is quite foreign to a great many members of this group. They are quite content to accept things given to them (if they deem the gift worthy enough to accept at all) and believe reciprocating in kind to be an antiquated idea. For a Gen X, the thought of not reciprocating is unthinkable, so it is easy to see how battle lines are very easily drawn on this issue. The wise leader is aware of the division with respect to the Law of Reciprocity and takes great pains to educate and prevent unspoken resentment from building.

We have all read page after page of opinion and testimony making leaders responsible for adaptation of their styles and systems to foster safety and creativity for their colleagues and employees. Today it is Generation X and the older Millennials that are creating new systems and adapting their styles to meet the needs of the younger portion of Generation Y and the first of Generation Z. When time and tide create the situation whereby Gen Y and Z must create appropriate work places that include employees from Gen X, will it be just as difficult and complicated to adapt their beliefs to meet the needs of every individual in their employ?

Needs of Generation Z

In July of 2014, Anne Kingston wrote a piece called, *Get Ready for Generation Z*, and shared in via social media. In it, she spoke of the power of this latest generation to hit the job market. A portion of her paper is seen below:

"They're smarter than Boomers, and way more ambitious than the Millennials. Research, though still in beta, points to the emergence of a stellar generation: educated, industrious, collaborative, and eager to build a better planet. In fact, Gen Z is already being branded as a welcome foil to the Millennials, born between 1980 and the mid- or late 1990s, who have been typecast as tolerant but also overconfident, narcissistic and entitled. Those characteristics weren't an option for the first post-9/11 generation, one raised amid institutional and economic instability, informed by the looming shadow of depleting resources and global warming, and globally connected via social media."

A Sparks & Honey presentation offered the following: *"'Meet Generation Z: Forget everything you learned about Millennials,' said that "60 % of Gen Z wants jobs that have social impact, compared with 31% of Gen Ys. It deemed them entrepreneurial (72% want to start their own businesses), community oriented (26% volunteer) and prudent (56% said they were savers, not spenders. Gen Z is also seen to be more tolerant than Gen Y of racial, sexual, and generational diversity, and less likely to subscribe to traditional gender roles."*

Social researcher Mark McCrindle, of McCrindle Research said, *"They are the most connected, educated, and sophisticated generation in history. They don't just represent the future, they are creating it. The defining characteristic, so far, is that they're a new species: Screenagers, the first tribe of "digital natives.""*

Nikki Sun, senior student and marketing enthusiast at Babson College share her opinion in December 2015, again via social media:

"Gen Z's are radically different from previous generations because they were born into an age of technology and only know a life with the internet. While Millennials share their lives on social media, Gen Z's live and breathes through social media, often saying "if you didn't post it, it didn't happen." They are constantly connected to the digital world, digesting content every

minute of the day and aware of every move that their friends make. With multiple mobile devices, Gen Z's have mastered the art of multi-tasking, as they can be having a conversation with a parent while texting a friend and snap-chatting in between.

Gen Z's aren't interested in being mainstream. They embrace diversity and desire to be different, unique, and the first to find the new trend. Being tech savvy, they are experts at using the internet as a tool to research and treasure hunt. Endless amounts of information provide endless opportunities, leading to an especially creative and entrepreneurial generation. Social media platforms like Instagram have influenced this generation to be extremely visual. They are experience-driven, drawn to aesthetically pleasing Go-Pro photos and beautiful cinematography through short videos. Curious about the lives of others, they follow famous influencers to tap into aspirational lifestyles. Gen Z's are thrifty, as they do not spend large amounts of money on expensive brands. After watching their parents and older siblings struggle to find jobs during the recession, Gen Z's became value conscious and independent."

It is interesting to note that the Kingston and Sun articles were written by members of the Gen Z community, with that word, "community," being chosen deliberately. Pride in the accomplishments and attitudes of the generation is clearly defined by the authors, and justifiably so. Individuals of this group were born with the usual umbilical cord and a figurative electrical cord to power all their electronic devices. Constant contact with global information has led to a continual tidal wave of data for processing. They are masters of analysis and have been wading through oceans of tainted and biased information since birth, the happy consequence being that they, more than any other generation, are able to cut through the floating debris to find the pearls of truth.

They almost sound too good to be true, but as with all generations, they have their own baggage to bear:

Anxiety – The human brain develops in stages. As we age, we become more capable of understanding increasingly complex information. In the early stages of development, we are completely solipsistic, believing ourselves to be the center of the universe around which all else exists to fulfill our needs. For example, newborns cannot feel empathy or understand negative emotions such as hate, and a 2-year-old cannot comprehend sexual attractiveness. Even with parental controls in place, Generation Z has been bombarded with information beyond their developmental levels, the result being anxiety over the state of the world. Because they are so astute and involved in social media, they care deeply, but are not in positions to affect significant change. Yet. This is cause for duress and heightened anxiety. Additionally, they far prefer texting to speaking, and person to person communication and rapport is in decline.

To them, the telephone app on their cell phones is more decoration than much else; they far prefer to use the shorthand of the keyboard. This abbreviated communication leaves little space for sharing emotion, so anxiety over personal connection is growing. Social anxiety is being diagnosed much more frequently, and it is not uncommon to see ulcers in children of 8 and 9 years old.

Shortened Attention – The pace of the world, especially in business, has been picking up speed for quite a while, and technology has catapulted us into constant mental rush hour traffic. The pros and cons of multi-tasking have been debated, and not unexpectedly, the predominantly left brained men have come down on the negative side, and the predominantly right-brained women on the positive. (I personally believe that while no two thoughts can occur at exactly the same time, they can be ordered and overlapped to enable multiple ideas to converge into an illusion of multi-tasking.)

It doesn't really matter anymore whether multi-tasking meets with approval or not; Generation Z has been doing it since birth and for them it is as automatic as breathing. To create an analogy, in the past, some of us have had directed laser-like focus, with others of us more closely resembling disco balls. Gen Z combines the glittering characteristics of disco balls with laser-strong flashes of intense focus in each sparkling glint.

They are intense for a moment, and then something else requires a brief moment of completely focused attention and then another, and another. They are the perfect personified picture of Shiny Object Syndrome or, said another way, "Squirrel!" Their spans of attention are short, dedicated, and directed (strongly resembling that of a Cocker Spaniel puppy) in order to juggle data and prevent informational and emotional overload. Even during periods of rest, Gen Z will be watching a screen for one show, while listening through headphones to another, while texting a friend about what they just saw or heard; the only way they can accomplish such feats of multi-tasking is to absorb information quickly and completely for a brief second, and then move on to the next item demanding their attention. This can, of course, give rise to confusion causing the individuals' anxiety to rise (see Anxiety, above) whereupon they look to find answers using their most used resources of the internet and social media. How easy it is to find another shiny squirrel there, and the process begins anew.

Generation X The Cowboys	Generation Z The Diversifiers
Lost Generation, latchkey kids took greater responsibility for raising themselves	Helicopter parents always providing safety net for their children
Independence is highly valued and actively sought.	Community, diversity, and tolerance hold high value.
Skeptical, preponderance of "What's in it for me" attitude	Globally involved, desiring global impact, but still wanting instant gratification
Will perform duties as requested by leaders and bosses	Will go beyond requested duties
Reached adulthood during difficult economic times	Raised amid financial instability, depleting resources, and global warming. Financially frugal
Little value for loyalty	Globally connected and loyal to creating a better world.
Cynical, pessimistic, questioning of conventionality	Accustomed to diversity, value transparency, and freedom of choice
Want to paid well; willing to work their way up through the ranks	Want to be paid well; they know their skills are a valuable commodity
Great concern over family vs. work	Global connectivity leads to concern for the planet
Need flexibility and challenge at work	Multi-tasking masters, in need of constant updates.
Respond well to few rules and opportunity for individuality	Demand teamwork and collaboration, and embrace diversity

SPECIAL NEEDS IN BUSINESS

Since the 1970s, schools have made an effort to serve students with "special needs." Prior to that time, students experiencing difficulty with the curriculum were given as much extra attention as the teacher could/would provide, and any behavior problems arising from student frustration was "solved" via physical punishment, aka, "the strap."

If these two measures didn't solve the problem, the child was labeled a slow learner, or was simply branded as being "bad," and in many cases, written off as unable to be successful in life, the universe, or anywhere. They may have been held back to repeat a year of schooling, resulting in their peers labeling them the social pariahs of the school yard. Inappropriate behaviors would escalate, their self-esteem would take a serious beating, and the previous assumptions of lack of possible success would prove themselves true. Parents were helpless as they had no power over the school's systems and methods, and were, in many cases, too frightened of authority to question the treatment of their child.

As it does, the pendulum has swung to parents claiming full authority over the way their children are treated, and teachers and administrators striving to keep everyone happy. Where there once were a handful of "special needs" students, today it seems that every individual has some special need or other. It doesn't stop at graduation, either. We have gone from children being seen and not heard, to becoming a full-blown "child-centric" society with youth demanding (and receiving) special attention at every turn.

Business leaders are reeling from the new situation not knowing how to handle this new breed of employee. I don't know when and where the middle of the pendulum swing was, but clearly the momentum was too powerful to let it stop in a happy middle position. (So, something else is new?)

The needs of individuals have always needed to be considered; neither end of the pendulum swing of too much vs. too little attention is appropriate and although we strive for some sort of equilibrium, the human race has yet to pull it off with any degree of success or permanency.

Through the ages though, there is one group of special needs individuals who have never demanded, and therefore never received any particular consideration to aid them in their search for success: our over-achievers. These are the kids that received Honors grades throughout school, who went on to higher education or who started businesses. The ones who got away with a little bit of naughty because they could figure out how to do it without being caught, and the ones who knew how to take calculated risks and still come out ahead of the game.

These individuals rarely receive any extra help because they don't ask for it, but just because they are successful within the limits of their knowledge doesn't mean they wouldn't do even better with even a modicum of assistance. These people, the bright and the curious, the spirited and the adventurous are as much "Special Needs" as the individuals with learning difficulties or physical handicaps.

Before anyone gets riled and ready to assault me in a dark alley, be reassured that I am not denying that people with difficulties need and merit extra help; we absolutely must do everything we can to ensure they experience success to the absolute peak of their potentials. What I am saying is that we must also provide our high achievers with the same consideration. Furthermore, while special tutors, classroom aids, and psychologists are trained and ready to help the more usual special needs individuals, it is far more difficult for the overachievers to find mentors and teachers to help them reach their highest limits.

Let's bring this into the world of business. We are in an era in North America, where the majority of the workforce has been raised absolutely knowing they are "special." This group is currently wearing the labels of pampered, entitled, spoiled, and so on. In fact, they are behaving exactly as they should, given the nature and circumstances of the world into which they were born. This group has more "special needs" than any before; at home and at school they were taught they were destined for greatness, that they were special, and that there would always be a safety net to catch them should they fall. They are demanding, particular, and will not abide the workplace hierarchies that have served us in the past.

They are also brilliant and they do have special needs, including the highest achieving of them.

In the business world, these individuals can only reach their heights of accomplishment through a mentoring process. Herein lays the problem: who is qualified to take on that role?

We are in a rapid state of change. Technology has altered the systems we once used for building successful businesses, and continues to do so with every day that passes. The mailroom, so often used as the icon of the bottom rung of the corporate ladder, no longer even exists. Standard business hours of 9-5 are almost obsolete, and meeting with overseas partners is now done with parties happily ensconced in their home offices. For some, these are new-fangled procedures, but to the up and comers, they are already old news; they have never known the world without these technological advantages.

Yet, to be successful, they need to understand what has been to project and plan for what can be. They need to be taught, but they are reticent to ask for help because to do so would signify a gap in their brilliance. They need guidance, but they are so accustomed to having their every whim fulfilled even without asking, they don't understand that they must request assistance.

When any one of us needs assistance, who do we ask? Like as not, we turn to individuals we trust to not judge us as ignorant, to those with experience, or to those with reasoning skills to help us sort out the problem. We may look for a sympathetic ear, or a wise sage, or a guide-on-the-side. Even if the exact solution may not be forthcoming, we look for those who might provide a different perspective, or an additional bit of background knowledge.

The solutions may be only a question or conversation away, but the crux of the problem is that the question must be asked or the conversation invited, and the current generations are in a bit of a pickle with that. Asking for assistance can be a double-edged sword for the mighty and brilliant: all their lives they've seen their "special needs peers" asking for help; will they be branded as "needy" simply through the asking? Or will they be rebuffed and scorned by the old-world hierarchy resorting to, "information on a need to know basis only?"

A brilliant brain and a high-level education do not necessarily contribute to quality emotional education, and ego still plays a big part in the success formula.

All of this can be addressed in some measure with existing business leaders making the first move to create workplace environments where it is safe to ask questions, and where "bosses" are replaced with "mentors". If toes are curling with the nerve of that affront to the status quo, then the point has been made. Our new brilliant minds are the leaders of the future, and are very much "special needs."

The time to address their special needs has long since passed, and the situation has become undeniable. The current generation is the bridge between the outdated systems of the past and the new dynamic business models of the future, and they cannot do it alone. Current business leaders must rise to the challenge of providing a guiding hand, some direction, and most of all, a listening ear to carry the world of business into the bright and adventurous future that is still being invented by this important Special Needs group.

IN A NUTSHELL

Boomers I - Prestige conscious, they enjoy public recognition and they value individualism and self-expression.

Boomers II - Personal gratification and public recognition are highly valued.

Generation X - They respond well to, "There aren't a lot of rules," and, "Do it your way."

Generation Y – Give them systematic feedback and allow them input into all things in which they participate. Send them messages that stress team spirit. 9-5 hours hold no interest for them. Allow flexible work schedules. Key words are: collaborate, connect, co-create, and teamwork.

Generation Z – Like the Millennials, this group is driven by instant gratification, and believe that success is a given. They believe in being of service to others, and they will not abide leadership through intimidation or displays of physical power. They have information on their side, were raised in an atmosphere of, "It's cool to be smart," and know full well that they, "know more," than their bosses. Health of body, mind and soul is important to them. Treat them as valued members of the team.

It is not enough for only the leader to understand what each generation needs to be successful. It is equally important, and perhaps even more so, that each generation acknowledge the strengths and weakness of their counterparts. That means that not only does Generation X need to accept the needs of Generation Y and Z, but that the same understanding must be reciprocated by Y and Z and directed back to X.

Tailor messages for generational preference. Feedback, instruction, and information must be continuous. This will be difficult for the independent Gen X individuals; mutual trust must become Job 1.

Educating employees on the values of the various generations will improve corporate culture, attract talent across generations, improve employee morale and engagement, reduce age discrimination, and result in better employee retention. Employees are not necessarily aware of the core values of each of the generations, so to improve corporate culture, they must be taught.

Shining the light on **why** there are tensions and clarifying understanding through education will create a culture of acceptance and respect, thereby resulting, again, in better employee retention and a more productive environment.

Create programs that encourage generations to work together and share knowledge. Older generations have traditionally preferred to work independently while younger generations thrive in an atmosphere of teamwork and transparency. Closing generational gaps requires building a culture of acceptance and respect which can be initiated by creating diverse teams wherein the strengths of individuals are required and celebrated.

Leaders must model the attitude of respect for each generation's strengths and create a culture of mutual respect. They must also model flexibility in their styles and encourage their management teams to do the same. Some generations resent micro-management techniques while others prefer more instruction. Help your management team learn to recognize and address employee needs.

Business leaders are only as successful as their followers. By understanding and fulfilling the needs and values of each of the generations, they will realize greater success than by using the broad leadership strokes of the past. This may sound like an onerous task, but be reassured in the knowledge that there is plenty of cross-over between the generations. Find those points of intersection and build on them.

SUMMARY

It is not the strongest of the species that survive, or the most intelligent, but the one most responsive to change.

~ Charles Darwin

Young people push boundaries! It is what each generation before them has done and it is right to do so. The pendulum swings from one extreme to another moving quickly from children being seen and not heard, to becoming the epicenter of their parent's lives. Perhaps it will swing back the other way in years to come. For now, however, it is wonderful to see the confidence of this breed of humans. We have taught them to be unafraid of trying new things, of looking for new and easier ways to accomplish everything, to set goals and believe they can reach them.

Yes, it is difficult to lead and "manage" people who know more than we do, and yes, they do things differently than we did. We changed the world when our generation came on the scene, and now we can help the Millennials and Gen Z change it again. Be proactive. Mentor them. Guide them. They have great potential, and with our help and support, perhaps this will be the generation that truly makes our world the best place it can be.

CHAPTER 3

Disruption Leadership

There is only one way to get anybody to do anything.
And that is by making the other person want to do it.

~Dale Carnegie

I t used to be that the goal for organizations was stability. We wanted predictable earnings via modest modifications, prices kept in check, and people that stayed in their jobs. Thanks to market transparency, labor mobility, global capital flows and instant communication leading to heightened global competition, leaders are now intensely concentrated on change.

There is an excellent video on YouTube that clearly demonstrates the changes happening in the modern workplace.

You might enjoy watching it:

Inno-Versity Presents: "Greatness" by David Marquet

www.youtube.com/watch?v=OqmdLcyES_Q

Whether business or personal, change causes distress and distressed employees are not productive employees.

Today, not only do leaders need to be strategic and tactical, in order to succeed, they also must have intimate understanding of the human side of change management i.e. *the alignment of company culture, values, people, and behavior.* For change to be successful, it must occur at the level of the individual employee just as deeply as it does at leadership levels.

Change is inevitable and it is happening faster than ever before. To cope and survive and thrive, when faced with change wherever it occurs, true leaders become energized rather than paralyzed and help others to do the same.

NUDGE THEORY

Significant changes in business will always lead to, "people issues." A tool that has been used under different names and for different purposes is called the **Nudge Theory.** It is a powerful change-management concept which emerged in the early 2000s. It can be very useful in understanding and managing change, especially where resistance among people seems strong, and conventional approaches are failing, or causing conflict.

Nudge theory is mainly concerned with the design of choices which influences the decisions we make:

- Understanding of how people think, make decisions, and behave
- Helping people improve their thinking and decisions
- Managing change of all sorts
- Identifying and modifying existing unhelpful influences on people

What the theory seeks to do is to improve understanding and management of influences of human behavior which is central to "changing" people and their attitudes. Central to behavioral and attitudinal change is an understanding of how decisions are communicated. It is based on indirect encouragement and enablement so it avoids direction instruction or enforcement.

Do you remember Mary Poppins? The very first thing Mary Poppins does is to nudge the two children in her charge into cleaning the nursery:

"In every job that must be done there is an element of fun. You find the fun, and Snap, the job's a game,"…thereby nudging the children into happily accepting the task of tidying up the room.

Similarly, by making their vitamins suitable to each child's taste in, "*Just a Spoonful of Sugar Helps the Medicine Go Down,*" not only did she become an agent of change, she showed the children the benefits of the change, thereby making them eager to embrace other possible changes in the future.

At no time did the children have any choice in their situations, but by showing them the benefits of accepting change, their fear and resistance disappeared in short order. We are not children, nor are we so easily swayed from our opinions, hopes or fears. Nevertheless, the analogy holds true for adults in business just as well as for the children in the movie.

Enforce	Nudge
Instruct a child to tidy his/her room	Play a room tidying game with the child
Erect signs: No Littering: $200 fine	Improve availability and visibility of trash bins
Join a gym	Use the stairs
Count calories	Use a smaller plate
Create a weekly food shopping budget	Use a basket instead of a shopping cart

The Nudge Theory is really about shifting the frame of reference. Consider two different ways of presenting bad news. There was a perfect example on social media that spoke of a university in Colorado having trouble getting the grass to grow on campus because the students kept walking on it.

They tried signage saying, "Do Not Walk on the Grass," but the message was ignored and the grass kept getting trampled. The university opted to take a different approach with signs reading, "Give Earth a Chance." Like magic the students stopped walking on the grass. The university simply changed the perspective of its students by making the issue an environmental one.

Enforce	Nudge
Require on-going professional development	Provide in-house training during business hours
Impose deadlines for tasks	Discuss reasonable dates for completion
Expect attendance at budget meetings	Cater the budget meetings
Limit sick days	Offer discounted memberships to gym
Limit vacation times	Offer incentives to work during peak periods

Through Nudging, the employee is persuaded that there is benefit to them as well as being in the best interest of the company to acquire ongoing professional development, to meet deadlines, attend budget meetings, to maintain good health, and to work during the busiest seasons. Employee and employer work together to meet the goals of the company, and a pleasant culture is maintained.

When change is due, nudging can be used to allow individuals to see and understand the benefits of the change. Regardless of the generation, people accept change more readily when they are clear about the reasons for it, the possible repercussions of it, and what its benefits will be, both to the company, and to themselves and their colleagues.

LAWS OF PERSUASION

Real persuasion comes from putting more of you into everything you say. Words have an effect. Words loaded with emotion have a powerful effect.

~ Jim Rohn

The art of persuasion is extraordinarily powerful and must be used with care. In business, leaders use it to influence decisions with clients, competitors and employees, and the careful use of it can be very effective when trying to "sell" change to people.

Persuasion techniques must be used ethically; motivating and encouraging people to apply a positive and constructive approach to the challenges of change is completely acceptable, while distorting the situation so that it is made to look acceptable or even advantageous is not.

There are certain Laws of Persuasion (the number of which vary depending on the resource and the divisions) most commonly used in sales and marketing, but which are equally effective when ethical persuasion must be used to help individuals accept change.

The Law of Reciprocity

The most important single ingredient in the formula of success is, knowing how to get along with people.

~Theodore Roosevelt

The Law of Reciprocity says that when someone receives a gift they perceive to be valuable, they immediately feel an urge to, "return the favor." If someone does something nice for you, you consciously or subconsciously look for ways to do something nice in return. It works in reverse as well: if you do something nice for someone, you expect them to favor you in kind, at some point, and in some way. If a leader makes an effort to make an individual feel special and valued, it is usually repaid with loyalty and an increased desired to prove the leader was right to hold that positive opinion. Conversely, if an employee diligently applies himself to completing an assignment or task in record time and with extraordinary quality and does **not** receive a commendation from the leader, he will feel affronted and resentful at the lack of what he feels to be rightfully owed attention; the Law of Reciprocity was not fulfilled, and the debt not paid.

The "favor" bank can be "stacked" to some degree before repayment must be made, but nonpayment is not optional without feelings being hurt and relationship damage being done. The leader who makes a point of giving and repaying kindness, sympathy, and caring to his/her followers will have gone a long way to establishing a bond of trust, and will be able to persuade them much more easily than a leader who has ignored this unspoken law.

When speaking of the generation gaps in business, the Law of Reciprocity is an important one because within it lays one of the largest misunderstandings. Generation X and older are **bound** to this rule, and it governs much of their personal and professional behavior. Generation Y and Z do not live by this rule, and for the most part, are not even aware of its existence. Because these generations do not experience the urge to reciprocate, or at least not at the same levels of the Boomers and Gen X, favor and kindness debts awarded to the Millennials and Gen Z are not given a second thought by the recipients. Baby Boomers and Generation X live, eat, and breathe reciprocity, and when no repayment arrives, they tend to experience a flood of negativity toward the recipient of their gift, and the seeds of resentment and distrust are planted.

On the other side of the equation, Gen Y and Z are not as uniformly bound by the need to reciprocate and for the most part, are not even aware that any obligation is attached to kindness, favors, or gifts. When they provide those services to others, including the older generations, they expect nothing in return. They are more likely to accept the feel-good emotions that accompany their generosity to be payment enough. It is rare to find Gen Y and Z individuals doing something nice for someone because they want to stock up their favor bank, and think the whole system of 'owing a favor back' to be inane and silly.

Astute business leaders who are aware of this dichotomy of values can preempt this gap of understanding by addressing the issue as part of their business culture processes. As in most instances, drawing awareness and supplying education in the form of mentoring is the most effective means to a "gapless" workplace. Explanations of the expectations of reciprocity by each generation to each generation, is a good place to start.

The Law of Contrast

I have with me two gods, Persuasion and Compulsion.

~ Themistocles

The Law of Contrast states that when two items are different, a person will see them as even more diverse if they are placed close together. In the world of sales, the Law of Contrast decrees that the sale of the high-ticket item be completed before the salesperson may move into "upsell mode;" it also decrees that the upsell be done immediately following the initial deal.

A car sales agent would never sell a great set of car mats to a customer before first selling the car. A men's clothing store clerk will not encourage the customer to purchase a beautiful tie until after she/he first sells the suit. Even if the car mats or the tie are quite expensive, in comparison to the cost of the car or the suit, the price seems reasonable, and their value, high. Why wouldn't you protect your brand-new car with the set of mats? It seems silly to buy a beautiful suit and then not complete it with the silk tie. To allow the Law of Contrast to work for the sales representative, though, the car mats or the tie must be offered before the customer walks out the door so that the contrast in price is obvious and alluring.

The Law of Contrast holds sway over all the generations, however Generation Y are the most easily convinced by it. This group is used to being pampered; they feel entitled to receive the very best. Of Gen X, Y, and Z, they have the most limited financial awareness. Generation X's were raised in an era of prevailing scarcity; it is much more difficult to convince them to make a purchase in the first place, and they are highly skeptical of after-purchase additions. Once the decision to buy is made, though, it is pure logic that dictates that protection and enhancements are necessary. This is the generation that grew up with expensive furniture that was always covered with plastic in order to keep it in pristine condition for, "special company."

Like Generation Y, Gen Z has been raised by helicopter parents looking after their every need, and in a perfect world, they too, would like to receive the best of everything nicely wrapped up with a bow. The difference, however, is that Generation Z is concerned that the bow may end up taking space in a landfill, and that it was produced in a factory where workers are not fairly compensated for their labor. They would rather do without the extras if their globally-conscience compass remains steady. All their conditions being met however, Gen Y is affected by the Law of Contrast as much as any other group.

How does this 'law' affect the modern business world and its inherent generation gaps? It stands to reassure leaders that when 'selling' change of any kind inside an organization, they must first address the big-ticket items before detailing the smaller ones. If the business is to undergo a complete reorganization, people of all generations need to understand the big picture before they will buy into it. After the car is purchased then the discussion of the floor mats can occur; if the reorganization is accepted, then the specific details of what exactly will change can be more easily digested. Since Gen Y and Z are more accustomed to rapid and continual change, they are more open to being persuaded of its validity. Gen X is much more sensitive to maintaining the status quo, and information about changes must be clear, complete, and ongoing for them to feel secure, and thus, content.

The Law of Association

It's not the situation. It's your reaction to the situation.

~ Bob Conklin

Have you ever gone to see a movie you know little about just because you like the actor? Have you noticed how many car owners tend to stay within a certain manufacturing line, e.g. Ford, Toyota, Audi? That people that purchase Heinz ketchup also tend to buy Heinz mustard?

This is the Law of Association. If we liked Hugh Jackman in one movie, the next one he films will be enjoyable, too. We believe that if one Ford car was a great purchase, another Ford car will be equally good, and if we find Heinz ketchup to be tasty, Heinz mustard will also be delicious.

Excellent public speakers use the Law of Association via their use of space. Positive comments will always be made from one side of the space, negative comments from the other, and the call to action from a point in between. The world of advertising uses famous individuals to endorse products so as to shower the product with the individual's status; we like or respect the individual, therefore we like or respect the product. All of our 5 senses are easily activated via the Law of Association and it is an extremely powerful tool.

The Law of Association comes into play when we are rushed into making decisions or in the face of little other evidence on which to base our judgments. Before a job candidate has the opportunity to even say hello, the Law of Association has already provided evidence for the employer to form an opinion. If the candidate is dressed in a casual state, by association our perception is that he is probably not suitable for upper management or leadership rules. If the individual speaks using colloquialisms and mispronounces words, those roles are ruled out as well.

Bringing it home to the world of business, leaders must be careful to be associated with positivity and confidence and that can "look" different to Generation X, Y, and Z. Where Generation X sees a business suit to be a sign of authority, Generation Y may see it to be artificial and Generation Z may not care about it either way.

If the leader is consistently sincere in acting in the best interests of his/her employees, the association is that he/she can be trusted. Generation X will respect a leader if the color of his/her office is from the cool pallet with warmer colors reflected in the decorations. Generation Y needs to know that the leader is up-to-date and flexible, so the office décor must reflect that ideal. Generation Z is more conservative than Generation Y but not as strict as Generation X and the surroundings might be strong colors with warmer accents to associate the leader as both powerful and caring.

The one universal association that does not change from generation to generation is that everyone always has, and always will, want to be seen and heard; leaders who know how to genuinely listen to their followers will forever be associated with sincerity and good will.

The Law of Connectivity

When you make others feel good, they tend to gravitate to you.

~Tim Sanders

We have all met people with whom we seem to instantly connect, and others who immediately repel us. This is the Law of Connectivity. The Law of Connectivity states that the more we feel connected, part of, liked by, or attracted to someone, the more persuasive they become.

There are 4 components of this law: attraction, similarity, people sills, and rapport, none of which are possible without sincerity and a true interest in the other person.

Attractive people, simply by the virtue of being attractive, are deemed to be smarter, kinder, and more compassionate than average or below average-looking people. It's called the "halo" effect, and it makes people want to please the individual, feel inclined to place higher emphasis on every positive thing they do, and to forgive any "mistakes" they may make. We are subconsciously persuaded that their attractiveness applies to more than their physical attributes, and that their values and beliefs must be attractive too, thereby causing us to become much more open to liking them. Attractive people have an easier job of persuading others to their point of view.

Babies begin to "mirror" their caregivers very early in their lives; smiles beget smiles, frowns beget frowns. Mirroring continues throughout life with positive individuals drawing other positive individuals, and vice versa, and it is not restricted to facial clues or body language; we connect more easily to others that dress as we do, participate in the same activities, listen to the same music, and so on.

The Law of Connectivity is why leaders today are finding success in bridging the generation gaps by creating strong business cultures. The feeling of belonging and shared values created in working environments mimics the attributes of "family" and rapport, creating bonds that can withstand change, disruption, and even some failures. At the head of this "family" is the business leader. None of the generations are looking for a "father figure" per se, but they do want someone who will mentor them, lead them to improvement, and defend them when things go wrong, and the creation of a strong business culture is step one in the process.

The Law of Likeability

"People prefer to say 'yes' to those they know and like. People are also more likely to favor those who are physically attractive, similar to themselves, or who give them compliments. Even something as innocent as having the same name as your prospect, client, leader or follower increases the (effect of the Law of Likeability)."

~ Cialdini

This law is sometimes included in the Law of Connectivity, but for the sake of clarity, it can be considered in its own right. When we like people, we enjoy saying yes to them. We also say yes to people to cause them to like us. It has also been said that we say yes to people we would like to emulate. (This is the grown-up version of mirroring.)

It is not enough for a leader to have a brilliant vision and the technical skills required to create that vision. A leader is only as strong as his/her followers allow, and the more likeable the leader, the more people are willing to follow.

The Law of Esteem

I can live for two months on a good compliment.

~Mark Twain

The deepest principle of human nature
is the craving to be appreciated.

~William James

There are scant few individuals that do not want, and in fact, need praise, recognition, and acceptance. It doesn't make any difference whether we are young, old, rich, poor, leader, or follower; we all want to know that in some way, we are special. We all want to be accepted, we want to be respected, and we all want to feel worthy.

There is no generation gap here.

A true and sincere compliment has enormous power. Empty compliments will very quickly destroy trust and reduce credibility, but voicing genuine appreciation of others will elevate their spirit and result in increased effort to prove the validity of the praise. Great leaders know their ultimate responsibility is to create other great leaders, and the Law of Esteem is their most powerful tool.

The Law of Expectancy

In the long run, men hit only what they aim at. Therefore, they had better aim at something high.

~ Henry David Thoreau

The very best example of the Law of Expectancy came out of the wars. Morphine was the pain suppressant of choice for the hundreds and thousands of injured soldiers, but when supplies ran out, medical personnel needed to exercise the Law of Expectation. Patients in excruciating pain were given nothing more than saline solution but told they were receiving morphine. Data tells us that over 25% of the patients experienced a measurable reduction of suffering.

We tend to base decisions on expectations. If we are expected to accomplish a task, we try hard to meet those expectations in order to gain respect and improve our likeability. If we are expected to fail at that same task, we live up to that expectation as well. People will rise to the level of expectation, and fall to the level of doubt and skepticism.

Author John H. Spalding said, ***"Those who believe in our ability do more than stimulate us. They create for us an atmosphere in which it becomes easier to succeed."***

This law is a massive contributor to the width and depth of the generations gaps in 21st century business.

The Law of Expectancy says that expectations influence reality and create results. How many times then, are we to hear that Millennials are lazy, Millennials are entitled, Millennials are pampered, before we **expect** those characteristics and behaviors? Because expectations influence reality and create results, are we not validating and actually causing the generational stereotyping? If we expect Generation Y to behave like spoiled children on the playground that is what we will see. If we expect Generation X to be rigid and technophobic, we will see that, too. Dov Baron, a noted speaker and author, calls this seeing through "context lenses."

This speaks to two different but related tenets:

- We see want to expect to see, and
- We rise to the level of our confidence.

Stereotypes have never served anyone well, and the associated expectations created by them can be negatively destructive or supremely productive. Confidence can be destroyed or buoyed by those expectations. Without confidence in ourselves as leaders, we cannot lead others to find confidence in themselves, and without the confidence to succeed, we never will.

Racial prejudice, religious intolerance, and generational slander from any generation toward any other generation are all the result of the Law of Expectation and its power must be wielded with great care, including within the world of business. We also must protect ourselves from ourselves; the law of expectation can cause us to fall prey to our own beliefs that have been forged in this way, whether positively or negatively.

Strive to see with clear eyes, not "context lenses" tainted through possibly erroneous expectations.

The Law of Consistency

The easiest way to get someone to change their mind is to demonstrate that not changing would be inconsistent with who they are, what they believe in, and what they value.

Once we have come to a decision or formed an opinion, we don't like to change it. It is difficult enough to persuade people to another point of view even if their original position has never been shared with others, but once we say it aloud, or even more, write it down, we tend to become inflexible; no amount of evidence will persuade us to change our original opinion, even to the point of obstinacy and ludicrousness. This is the Law of Consistency and it is as personally binding as any contract.

Why do we become so immoveable and stubborn? Why do we feel so adamant that we must "save face" by sticking with an untenable position? One opinion is that it's simply easier to turn a deliberately blind eye to the possibility that we were always, or are now, in error, than to admit to the need for researching a new position, justifying the change to ourselves, and finally explaining those reasons to others.

People value consistency, and the older we get, the more we, "stick to our guns," making it increasingly difficult to create or adapt to change. Past performance is a remarkably reliable predictor of future performance, but periodically, generational values experience enough upheaval to force us to have a good long look at what we believe. It happened with the Baby Boomers and their, "sticking it to the man," attitude, and it is happening again with Generation Y and their, "I deserve more than starting at the bottom," point of view. Even so, once the adaptation is made and has a reasonable following, it becomes the new basis for consistency, and the process begins anew.

Consider that for many years, business was structured in a pyramidal form, with the wide base being the point of entry, and the apex representing the pinnacle of success. The individuals at the top of the pyramid worked long and hard to acquire the knowledge and skills to climb the steep and often slippery slopes, and it took tremendous dedication, sacrifice, and above all, time, to make the ascent. Everyone had to do it so it was deemed to be fair. Along come the "know it all" Millennials saying, "It may have taken 20 years for you to acquire your knowledge, but I have done it in a few months; why should I not be rewarded for what I can do now since I clearly don't have to put in the time to get there?" (Example courtesy of Dov Baron.)

It is completely true, but for those already having struggled up the side of the pyramid, it does not seem fair, so resentment rears its nasty head. Even when evidence of capability and knowledge are clearly indicated, the Law of Consistency makes it extraordinarily difficult for the older generations to change their mind about the need to, "put in the time, and pay the dues."

The Law of Social Proof

The greatest difficulty is that men do not think enough of themselves, do not consider what it is that they are sacrificing when they follow a herd.

~ Ralph Waldo Emerson

It is the rare individual who bases all their decisions on their own input alone. Many factors come into decision-making, one of the more powerful being the Law of Social Proof. This law is not generation specific but the pendulum of its importance swings not only within the generations, but also with the groups within those generations. There are and always will be Conformists, Nonconformists, and Contrarians and within these divisions can be seen the degree to which the actions and decisions of others (The Law of Social Proof) plays a part in our thinking processes.

Conformists are those individuals to whom "belonging" is highly valued, thereby giving enormous power to the Law of Social Proof. For these people, conformity equals security, and that security allows for confidence. When uncertain about a course of action, these individuals tend to look to their group, especially their peers, to guide their decisions and actions. Respect for, and compliance to the most commonly accepted social ideals and behaviors is the ruling tenet here, regardless of the generation.

At first glance, Contrarians may appear to be Nonconformists, but that is not the case. Contrarians do not follow generally accepted norms of behavior, true, but they tend to attract others to their different ideas, ending up with a group of people who conform to their nonconformity. Gangs are a perfect example of Contrarians. Although they may operate outside the law or social mores, they form their own rules of behavior within their groups. Participants willingly follow those rules, thereby conforming to their alternative situations. Their conforming behaviors run contrary to more acceptable ideas and behaviors, but they still conform to their group's enforced norms. In this group, The Law of Social Proof dictates that peer acceptance is more vital than almost any other value.

Nonconformists, more rare than Conformists or Contrarians, are individuals in every sense. These are the people who give little credence to the opinions of others. They don't look to others to guide their decision-making processes and they don't care how others react to their ideals or behaviors. The Law of Social Proof does not hold nearly as much sway here as it does for Conformists or Contrarians.

Generationally speaking, it was the Baby Boomers who caused chaos with their Contrarian ideas of, "Make love, not war," and fighting, "the system." Generation X was skeptical and tired of conflict, and therefore, reverted to more conformist thinking.

Millennials are much more dependent on the Law of Social Proof, sending messages and texts to their peers to help them make decisions. Generation Z is elevating the authority of the Law of Social Proof even more by not only conferring with their local and global peer groups, but with other generations as well.

In the work world, there are few true Nonconformists. Boomers and Generation X may see Gen Y and Z as Contrarians, but since Generation Y is currently the largest component of the work force, their beliefs will quickly become the new norm. The Contrarian Y and Z generations have now become the Conformists, and Boomers and Gen X, the least visible and influential of them all.

Regardless of the generation, in the business world of the 21st century, The Law of Social Proof is very powerful. Referrals, endorsements, testimonials, and references are all strong influences and leaders would do well to use them often as persuasion tools.

The Law of Authority

Before you are a leader, success is all about growing yourself. When you become a leader, success is all about growing others.

~Jack Welch

Once upon a time, a generation or two ago we would do almost anything if it was commanded by an authority. Elders, parents, teachers, police officers, lawyers, and so on, reigned by virtue of their age, knowledge, and experience. The boss in the office could have been the most diabolically devious and nefarious person ever to walk the Earth, but he was the boss so employees did his bidding. Sad, really.

To be an authority in today's business world is no longer dependent on age or status. For a company to respect their leaders, those individuals must be respected authorities in many more areas than in years past. To be a leader today demands subject expertise, tremendous business intelligence, and more and more, emotional intelligence. "Relationships" has become the key word for establishing authority, and the passé "chain" of command has evolved to become more of a circle of teamwork. It is not unusual to see leaders pass the baton of authority for a specific project to the most knowledgeable person on the team, and then accept it back once completion has been reached. This is only possible because trust has been established through relationships between the leader and his employees.

The following definition of the Law of Authority was once widely accepted:

People respect authority. They want to follow the lead of real experts. Business titles, impressive clothing, and even driving an expensive, high-performing automobile are proven factors in lending credibility to any individual. Giving the appearance of authority actually increases the likelihood that others will comply with requests – even if their authority is illegitimate.

The generational change of values is causing an erosion of this interpretation. To some degree, the corner office, the luxury car, and the expensive clothing are still symbols of status to the Baby Boomers, and Generation X, and even, although to a lesser degree, the earliest members of Generation Y, but people don't always work from offices anymore, or go to work in suits, or in some cities, even own a car at all.

Today, authority and leadership are not measured by these yardsticks or at least, not to the same degree, having been replaced by knowledge, technical skills, and people skills. The Law of Authority could now very easily read:

People respect the authority of individuals with subject expertise, the desire to mentor others to achieve their potential, and an appreciation for the contribution of others to the overall team. These factors being equal, the aura of authority can be enhanced through general appearance and charismatic presence.

The Law of Scarcity

Without a sense of urgency, desire loses its value.

~ Jim Rohn

The Law of Scarcity increases perceived value by limiting its availability. The last cookie in the jar is perceived to be more valuable than the first, especially if a sibling wants it too. Not only is it the last, but now it must be fought over or shared, because it is the last one. Its scarcity has increased its value. Even if that last cookie is not our favorite kind, by virtue of being the last one, we want it.

A single copy of a painting is far more valuable than a virtually identical copy, not only because of its artistry, but because of its scarcity. We want it so that no one else can have it thereby making both the painting and the sole owner, special. Additionally, after the artist dies, the painting again increases in value, once again due to the Law of Scarcity.

Businesses use this law as a fundamental economic standard because the Law of Scarcity and the law of supply and demand are strongly related. Ad copy quoting, "For a limited time only," or, "For the first 5 callers," or, "Quantities are limited," are enacting the Law of Scarcity.

Economics are the most major driver for the Law of Scarcity, and since the economics of the times influence peoples' values, at first glance it appears to be a generational swing. I believe that a stronger relationship is seen between scarcity and individuals with strongly competitive personalities; the generational comparison is an illusion owing to competition becoming more intense during economic downswings.

The importance of the Law of Scarcity is that, regardless of age, status, or generational values, perceived value rises dramatically when limitations on availability exist.

The Law of Involvement

Without involvement, there is no commitment.
Mark it down, asterisk it, circle it, underline it.
No involvement, no commitment.

~ Stephen Covey

The Law of Involvement dictates that the more individuals participate in creating a process, the more they commit to its success. Active engagement increases connection, and connection increases ownership, which increases commitment, which circles back to increasing involvement.

Excellent leaders know that by involving employees to contribute in finding possible solutions to a company problem, they become more willing to participate, thereby increasing ownership, commitment, and loyalty to both the company, and the leader. The problem now becomes their problem and the solution, their solution. People will support what they create.

The Law of Involvement used to be a rarity in business, primarily because the workforce didn't demand it. Generation X did not want to be involved in areas of the business that didn't directly relate to their role. They preferred information to be funneled so they could concern themselves with accomplishing their tasks very well and with pride. Leaders were happy to oblige, because a more democratic teamwork approach takes substantially more time than a cut and dried dictatorial system where few justifications for decisions were required.

Generation Y and Z will have none of that. They want to be involved. They want to know the why of every decision so they can do their part to support it. To not involve these groups is to open the door to let them leave, and since Millennials form the largest part of the workforce, this is a very risky scenario.

Boomers and Gen X viewed work as a means of paying for their more enjoyable pursuits. Standard Monday to Friday, 9-5 hours left evenings and weekend free for family and hobbies; work life and home life were separate entities, and they devoutly protested any intermingling. Business leaders began to struggle with work/life balance and if they wanted their companies to succeed, it was the "life" portion of the equation that took the hit. Stress became a popular and common word in everyone's vocabularies as we struggled to fulfill the demands of work and home.

The conditions of work have changed with the times, and today, Monday – Friday, 9-5 work applies to fewer and fewer people. Technology has made it possible to work outside of the office, and at any time of the day, and while it would be reasonable to think that involvement in company dealings might have decreased, in fact, the opposite has occurred.

Millennials want to belong, and they want to be involved. They want it so badly, that they are quite pleased to be needed and on-call 24 hours a day, 7 days a week. They don't want or need a separation between work life and home life and they are happy to do whatever is necessary to see a project through to completion, if only leaders involve them as valuable and needed members of the team. Giving this group responsibility and authority to do whatever is necessary to get a job done is high on their list of wants, and even more, very high on their list of needs. This is quite a change from their predecessors of Generation X and the Boomers.

Summary: Laws of Persuasion

Countless times we have heard the term, "spin it," referring to finding a positive "spin" on something that, at face value, appears negative. When speaking of mindset or limiting beliefs, this can be a strong and uplifting tool. However, when leaders use the "spin" technique to make change easier to manage by glossing over its effects on people, it amounts to nothing more than dishonesty. This is hardly a trait of a good leader. It may be done to avoid confrontation and debate, and doing so may make the change easier to install, but will ultimately lead to employee feelings of betrayal, and a subsequent explosion of emotion.

No matter the generation, people need to know what lies ahead, and to be consulted and supported in dealing with it. None of us likes nasty surprises, and dishonesty from leaders completely erases trust at the deepest level. Leaders have a fundamental responsibility to provide complete information and explanation to their followers and using persuasion techniques to convince them of facts skewed or biased to the leader's desired end is unethical and immoral.

That being said, used with integrity, the Laws of Persuasion are just as powerful today as they have ever been, and regardless of the generation is a hugely valuable asset in the leader's toolkit.

CHANGE LEADERSHIP

"You'll have people who start the fire. You'll have people who run away from the fire. Your job (as leader) is to run into the fire."

~ Robert E. Moritz

Change being the greatest threat to company efficiency, it falls to business leaders to understand how to quell fear, establish trust, and propel the employees to engage fully thereby producing excellent results.

It does not matter whether it involves adult or child, personal matters or business, the most usual reaction to change is to feel threatened and to become angry or to react with fear. As has been published in multiple places, it really boils down to 2 questions for most people:

Am I enough for the new situation?
Do I have enough for the new situation?

Am I enough? Will there be a place for me? Do I possess the knowledge and skills necessary to be successful?

Do I have enough? If there are new plans, targets, and roles to fill, do I have enough time to adjust? Will I be given tools and information to handle the new roles and responsibilities? Do I have enough money saved, enough energy to serve me to successfully find another position if I must?

If accurate information is shared quickly, we can then make decisions and check our emotions. If insufficient information is available, the rumor mill will quickly begin to turn, insecurities will rise, and emotions will run amok. Even more, if leadership offers only snippets of information to select people, any previous trust will quickly disappear and be replaced with suspicion and resentment.

Change is both a business journey and a very personal one. People spend many hours each week at work; many think of their colleagues as a second family. Individuals and teams need to know how their work will change, what is expected of them during and after the change, how they will be measured, and what success or failure will mean for them and those around them.

They want to know 2 things:

What's in it for me?
How will this affect me?

People will react to what they see and hear around them, and need to have as much clear and correct information as possible. They need to be involved in the change process as early and as completely as possible. Communication and ownership are a leader's greatest allies over upheaval. The most important consideration is how the change will affect the people, which in turn will affect the culture and success of the organization. George Bernard Shaw said;

"The single biggest problem with communication is the illusion that it has taken place."

Additionally, John Jones of the Harvard Business School said,

"Most leaders contemplating change know that people matter. It is all too tempting to dwell on the plans and processes, which don't talk back and don't respond emotionally, but the most important piece to engaging in any change is to face up to the more difficult and more critical human issues."

Everything changes

Some changes are easier than others.

Some changes are easier to take than others.

Consider the change you yourself instigate versus change that is forced upon you.

Some people accept change easier than others.

Some of us are clever enough to actively seek out change, weigh it, measure it, and come to a decision about it.

As leaders in business, it falls to us to make transformational change as efficient and painless as possible. This is not an easy task, and especially so since the nature of the workforce is presently in a state of flux. Leaders are expected to steer their businesses, guide their administrators and staff, mentor and train their successors, and have ready answers at their fingertips.

WORK CULTURES

If you want your people to think, stop giving orders. Give intent. It transfers the psychological ownership. Then ask them, "Is it the right thing to do?" They will then make decisions as if the CEO is right behind them. Move the authority to where the information is.

John Watson is a member of a movement begun by Gavin Larkin in Canberra, Australia, leading business leaders to create "R U O K? work cultures," striving to attend to the mental wellbeing of individuals in organizations. He cites evidence from conversations with Human Resource managers from the corporate, government, and not for profit sectors who believe that **change fatigue** is now consuming many workplaces. He is quoted as saying,

"Be kind. Everyone you meet is fighting a hard battle. I've learned that often behind the cheery façade of many people are daily battles."

He believes that this insight is essential for leaders to understand, "because in these volatile, uncertain, complex and ambiguous times, employees are under continual strain to do 'more with less.' Their minds are distracted with a million different things."

He further commented on a report detailing an ongoing Gallup research report on employee engagement. One of their findings revealed that the greatest positive predictor of an individual's engagement at work is their belief that if a supervisor or someone at work seems to care about them as a person, that single belief could be maintained by simply having leaders and colleagues regularly ask each other, "Are you OK?"

Following up by listening to the answer without judgment, while encouraging action and then following up later, would lead to feeling included and eliciting reciprocal action. The poll goes on to conclude, that, "Caring and compassionate leadership is good for people and good for business."

The changing attitude toward work and its relationship with the other aspects of our lives has led to a strong increase in the value of corporate cultures. Where work was once seen as a means to an end and a necessary way to pay for more pleasant pursuits, more and more, our work is becoming an extension of ourselves, our beliefs, and our values.

This change in attitude toward the way we spend approximately 40 hours a week, coupled with Gen Y and Z's itchy feet and belief that the work they do must be meaningful, has caused business leaders to very seriously investigate the ways and means of retaining good employees. In essence, leaders have to know how to keep their employees happy.

In December of 2016, HR consultant Cissy Pau, released an article discussing why and how smaller companies are more successful at keeping their employees, "happy and therefore more productive and engaged. In so doing, they are able to attract and retain talent, ultimately leading to greater company success. Her research led her to state that the happiest employees have pride in their organization, feel appreciated for the work they do, and are treated with fairness and respect."

She also cited that "the happiest employees are found in marketing and creative roles, their first year on the job, senior executive roles, the age 55+ bracket and/or companies with fewer than 10 people." That smaller companies were on the list was a bit of a surprise finding until Ms. Pau noted the following aspects:

- **Noticeable Contributions:** In small companies, everyone's contribution makes an immediate and noticeable difference. Employees succeed or fail based on their own contributions and merits.

- **Close working relationships:** Small businesses have the luxury of employees' being able to build close working relationships. Working with small businesses, we often hear that staff are treated like family, and people really know and care about one another.

- **Strong connection to purpose:** When businesses are small, it's often easy to understand the company's vision and what it wants to achieve. By having a strong understanding a company's purpose and being able to hear and see that you are working to fulfill that purpose makes for a much more rewarding job.

Assuming Ms. Pau's findings to be correct, and that appreciation for noticeable contributions, close working relationships and a strong connection to purpose lead to happier employees, it stands to reason that employees enjoying that culture would also adapt to change much easier than those without the security of "mattering."

It takes strong leadership to have created a close and RUOK? culture, so assuming that change is being instigated by that leader, the employees would already have the trust and belief in his/her ability to answer their questions of What's in it for Me? and, How will this affect me?

Robert E. Moritz, US Chairman and Senior Partner at PricewaterhouseCoopers shared an article via LinkedIn wherein he discusses what he sees as the 10 Guiding Principles for Change Management.

The following is adapted from that article:

People Issues: Employees will be uncertain and resistant. Planning a systematic and complete approach c/w a method to adapt it as necessary will provide assurance that the matter is in-hand. Piece-meal changes threaten the speed of the change, the results of the change, and staff morale at risk.

Take it From the Top: Support from the CEO and leadership team will be required.

Change is inherently unsettling for people. Leaders must fully embrace the change in order to provide strength, support and direction. They must present with confidence, in a unified voice, and model desired behaviors. It will be equally stressful for the leaders as their followers.

The Layer Cake: Design a "cascade" effect to implement change to each section of the organization. Leaders of each department must be identified and trained, aligned to the new vision, equipped to executive their specific mission, and motivated to make the change happen.

Testify: Customize the message for various internal audiences using terms that matter to the individuals within that audience. Provide a road map to guide behavior and decision making.

Ownership: Mere buy-in or passive agreement on the part of leaders will not suffice. They must whole-heartedly show support for the change. As often as possible, involve people in identifying problems and crafting solutions. Reward tangibly ($) or psychologically (camaraderie and a sense of shared destiny).

Communication: Solicit employee input and feedback even though this will require over-communication through multiple, redundant channels. Avoid the mistake of thinking that others understand the issues and new direction, or feel the need to change. Reinforce core messages regularly, in a timely and inspirational way.

Cultural Assessment: Identify core values, beliefs, behaviors, and perceptions in order to assess organizational readiness to change, bring major problems to the surface, identify conflicts, and define factors that can recognize and influence sources of leadership and resistance.

Address Culture: Culture is an amalgam of shared history, explicit values and beliefs, and common attitudes and behaviors, and it must be addressed thoroughly.

Prepare for the unexpected: Continually reassess the organization's willingness and ability to adopt the change by using personal and corporate values as the guide.

Make it personal: People will react to what they see and hear around them, and need to be involved in the change process. Sanction or removal of highly resistant people will reinforce the institution's commitment. Plans and processes matter. People matter more.

CHARISMA

"I've learned that people will forget what you said, people will forget what you did, but people will never forget how you made them feel."

~ Maya Angelou

Have you ever wondered what it is about some people that make others sit up and take notice of them just by entering the room? Why some of individuals seem to have an aura of warm power that makes others gravitate to them?

What we're really talking about here is charisma, and it is a critical business leadership skill.

Some people believe that charisma is something that the privileged among us are born with and the rest of us are simply out of luck. Not so. Charisma can be learned, honed, and turned on and off at will.

The story of Norma Jean Baker is well known but its message is strong so it bears repeating.

During a very busy time of day, Monroe brought a photographer with her into Grand Central Station in New York City. People were everywhere, yet no one seemed to recognize one of the most famous people in the world. She boarded a train and quietly rode to the next station without anyone noticing. Monroe was trying to prove a point that just by deciding to, she could either be glamorous, Marilyn, or plain Norma Jean Baker (her real name). On the subway, she was Norma Jean, but when she resurfaced on to the busy New York sidewalks, she decided to turn into Marilyn. She looked around and teasingly asked the photographer, "Do you want to see her?"

Then, with no grand gestures, she just fluffed up her hair and struck a pose. With this simple shift, she suddenly became magnetic. An aura of magic seemed to flow out from her and everything stopped. Time stood still, as did the people around her, who suddenly recognized the star standing in their midst.

Charisma has been studied by a great many people, and modern opinion is that anyone can learn it. There are books with tag lines as follows: "How anyone can master the art and science of personal magnetism," and so on.

What then, is charisma and why is it considered to be a critical business leadership skill?

Charisma is powerful. There is no doubt about it, and equally without doubt is that it can be learned, and turned on and off at will. It's a huge topic and a really good one if you want to be a Super Leader, so I encourage you to look into it in some detail. Charismatic leaders show respect to their followers by paying close attention to what they say. They know when people feel they are heard, they feel important. And they are important; just try being a leader without any followers.

Beyond the usual expectations of leadership lives the quality of leadership and that is where charisma comes into play. Again, some individuals come by this quality naturally, and others must learn it. Its magnetism is compelling, persuasive, and it can move mountains. It is powerful, it is magnetic, and it is vital.

Charisma has 3 components:

- Presence
- Power
- Warmth

Presence

Definition: Completely in the moment, focused on the now and with a powerfully magnetic personality that draws focus and followers

Irrespective of your designation, your industry, or your role, your presence is an important area of concern. Presence has a great deal to do with the trust people have in you, and ultimately, your success. Presence is how you land on others. It is the assessment others make of your impact on them. It is based on the body you show up in, and the emotional energy you emit generally, and in particular moments. Once you start to speak, what you say and how you say it also impacts your presence.

Power

Definition: The ability to instigate, control, and or change a situation

Warmth

Definition: Sympathetic, empathetic, and compassionate toward others

Charismatic leaders do have power, and they use it to enrich the world around them. They use their power to help others find and live up to their potential, thereby, in their opinion, bettering the world for all.

Charismatic leadership does not depend on the rightness or wrongness of the cause; as with all forms of leadership, it depends entirely on whether anyone will follow.

Using a scale of 1-5 with 1 being low and 5 being high, rate the individuals listed on the chart for Presence, Power, and Warmth.

NAME	PRESENCE	POWER	WARMTH
Dali Lama			
Justin Trudeau			
Donald Trump			
Nelson Mandela			
Adolf Hitler			

Positive charismatic leaders truly care about others. They celebrate the wins and empathize with the losses, thereby strengthening trust, and placing importance.

You might think that the strongest leaders would score high in all the categories, but in fact, that's not always the case. Left-brained people tend to score higher for Presence and Power. Right brained people tend to score higher for Warmth.

If strong leadership is the goal, charisma is the fast track to it, and it is a skill that can and must be learned.

"What if, and I know this sounds kooky,
we communicated with the employees."

COMMUNICATING WITH YOUR TEAM

Communication involves 3 stages: Speaking, Listening, and Action. Leaders really must get over their need to hear themselves speak and place far more importance on the listening part. Listening, on its own, is a good start, but if there is no resultant action, people will quite quickly stop talking. What would be the point of going on?

Leaders who understand and appreciate that, "The whole is greater than the sum of its parts," are the younger generations, "cup of tea." Generation Z have grown up in a world of global influence and in world-wide communities, consideration by and for the entire team, led by strong, approachable, and flexible leaders; for them, open and meaningful communication is the unavoidable first ingredient to business success.

Brent Gleeson offers these following 5 suggestions for communicating with your team:

Be present:

Business executives, entrepreneurs and leaders of all kinds usually have days with little to no downtime. We rush from meeting to meeting to conference calls, rarely taking the time to clear our heads and reset for the next item on our agenda.

Most studies show that humans are truly productive for on a few minutes each hour, mostly due to distractions. Whether you are chatting with a colleague in the break room, on a client call with other team members or leading a company meeting, be actively present in the moment. Be engaged with your audience no matter how trivial you think the conversation may be. That way they know you care.

Ask the right questions.

Some of the best advice I have ever received was simply about asking the right questions that will foster productive and intelligent communication between the team. As leaders, one of the greatest privileges we have is building a great team. Hopefully, one comprised of people much smarter and more talented than ourselves! If that is the case, why would we spend all our time giving directives and assuming we know more than most in the room? By guiding a conversation with a specific goal in mind, we accomplish much more by leveraging the talent surrounding us.

Speak less, listen more.

Similar to asking the right questions is to actively listen to those speaking. We often find ourselves in the bad habit of thinking about what we are going to say next as opposed to actually listening to the other people speaking. When we do that, we aren't truly engaged in the conversation. Leadership isn't about standing on a soap box shouting orders. You often notice that the wisest people listen more and speak less. The less we talk, the more we will learn from those around us.

Work on emotional intelligence.

This is a topic that can't be covered in one bullet point but worth mentioning because it is often overlooked or deemed an unnecessary quality. Emotional intelligence is not a softer-side leadership quality; it's imperative. Being self-aware, disciplined, empathetic, and remaining calm under pressure are all aspects of emotional intelligence that can improve leadership ability. These emotional competencies are not innate talents but rather learned capabilities that must be worked on and developed over time so get on it!

Stay calm and be positive.

Calm is contagious, and so is panic. Smile. Carry yourself with confidence and try not to wear your emotions on your sleeve. Be aware that effective communication is about 7% of the words we say. The rest is about body language, tone, and delivery.

Another well-known contributor to the new leadership paradigm is Mary Kelly who recently discussed how to create strong working relationships between leaders and followers. In it she pointed out that while asking questions to begin conversations was a good starting point, asking Stupid Questions was not, as illustrated in the following snippet:

"Are your leaders asking stupid questions? If they are, they will likely get stupid answers when they do get answers, and they will believe the answers. Leaders like the illusion that if they walk around and ask employees questions that generate single syllable answers, they are being a good leader. For many managers, this satisfies what they perceive as doing what they

need to do to find out what is really going on in the organization. They are wrong. Most organizational leaders ask questions that don't elicit any real information. These are common exchanges. Note that no real information is exchanged:

Leader: "Good morning. How are you?"
Employee: "Good!"

Leader: "How are things?"
Employee: "Great!"

Leader: "How is your day?"
Employee: "Fine."

The leader then returns to his or her office, satisfied that they have done their due diligence of MBWA (Management by Walking Around), self-assured that they have assessed the pulse of their workforce. Thus reassured, they determine that everything is fine.

Questions are an excellent start to having meaningful conversations, but the nature of the questions cannot be superficial. If a passing, "Good morning, how are you today?" is simply a greeting, then, "Fine," is a perfectly acceptable answer. If a true conversation is the desired outcome, then the question must be engaging, and unanswerable with a yes, no, or a one word answer. If leaders really want to know what is going on with their people, then they must understand three rules: first, they must create questions that will lead to meaningful answers, second, they must be prepared to actually listen to the answers, and third, they must have some means of responding to the answers.

Mary Kelly suggests the following questions:

- *What is the most interesting part of this project for you?*

- *Are there any parts of your boss's job that you think you'd like?*

- *What are you working on that makes you want to advance?*

- *How can this organization do to help you achieve your professional goals?*

- *What do you think we do around here that we should stop doing?*

- *From your perspective, what do we do that is wasting our employees' time?*

- *What can your team and I do to help you do your job better?*

- *If you could make one change to a policy here, what would it be?*

Asking engaging questions and receiving meaningful answers, amounts to nothing if no action is ever taken. As you can imagine, many leaders could well be threatened by the possibility of opening Pandora's Box.

It takes a great deal of confidence to be open to suggestions, and for this brand-new paradigm to work in this brand-new world of business, it also means the leader must relinquish control in order to create a culture of individuals working together with a common goal for a specific target. It requires that leaders have an enormous amount of trust for their team members, a deep appreciation of the benefits of teamwork, counsel from trusted advisors and mentors, and the willingness to be uncomfortable so as to increase the size of their personal and corporate comfort zones. Before any of that can begin to work though, the first absolute essential skill is, knowing how to communicate with others, in the language they understand, and listening and responding to their replies.

OUTCOME BASED THINKING

A very large responsibility of leadership is to create the environment for greatness. Start with Outcome Based Thinking. Known under a variety of names depending on the business, Outcome Based Thinking is the process of beginning with the end in mind. It is simple to understand using the analogy that if you know where you want to end up, you will find multiple roads to get you there. A perfect example is planning a family vacation:

Step 1: Decide you want to go on a holiday.

Step 2: Assign a length of time for the trip.

Step 3: Decide on a destination.

Step 4: Investigate and choose the mode of transportation, given the results of Step 2.

Step 5: Given the nature of the chosen holiday, and the ages, interests and needs of the family, select the best route to get you to your desired destination.

Step 6: Make arrangements for the care of your home while you will be away.

Step 7: Pack according to the needs of the family.

Step 8: Enjoy the trip.

Step 9: Return home, unpack, and get ready to return to work and school.

Without first deciding that you were taking a vacation, the planning process would have been impossible. Without setting the parameters for the vacation, further planning process would have been pointless. Without deciding on how you were getting to your destination, further steps would have…You get the point.

Transfer Outcome Based Thinking to your business. Without first knowing what our short and long term goals are, how can we make plans to reach them? Yet many leaders do not share their vision with sufficient passion and authority to excite and activate their followers to join the journey. Once we know our "destination," we are presented with all manner of "roads" that can take us there, and from that we can choose the paths that are best suited to our purpose.

Outcome Based Thinking is gaining popularity and acceptance by education curriculum specialists to more actively involve students in their own learning and the younger Gen y and most of Gen Z are accustomed to this planning process. Just as with technology, it is often useful to engage their skills and knowledge to help us through the difficult learning curves. Use them. They yearn to feel needed and the will not disappoint you when given the responsibility and the authority to lead a project of their own.

REACTIONARY VS PROACTIVE CHANGE RESPONSE

Our world is changing faster than most of us can keep up with. A stand-up comedian recently said, "If I could have one wish, I would ask the Geeks and Nerds of the Tech World to go on vacation for 6 months so the rest of us could catch up. Just take a break already!"

No one person can keep up with the foundational and technological activity and these extraordinarily wonderful advancements are both fantastic and frustrating. Some time ago, work in robotics removed the necessity of human beings standing mindlessly on assembly lines hour after hour and day after day. The people that lost their jobs weren't very happy, but the business world celebrated.

The days of Switchboard Operators came to a halt when technology opened that automation door, and again, while individuals earning their wages in that industry were negatively affected, business profits realized significant gains. The average person on the street doubtlessly feels helplessly buffeted by the gale force winds of change, and is in pure reactionary mode. Leaders, too, may feel helpless, especially if they are clinging to hierarchical business structures wherein they are, "lonely at the top."

To continue to be successful and profitable requires a team of dedicated individuals and in large corporations, a significant role of that leadership team is to become proactive agents of change. Just as the handle of a whip must move very little to make the tail travel fast and far, leaders that instigate small but strategic change will benefit from their powerful results. The status quo no longer exists and playing the part of the proverbial ostrich will not change that. Reactive responses can never be as quick or as effective as proactive instigation and excellent leaders must always be on the right side of that equation.

Generations Y and Z feast on change. Gen Z especially, has never known a world without constant and ongoing advancements, radical change, and excitement. It provides their daily fix of dopamine, their feel-good-juice, and it's all completely legal. Leaders that cannot keep up will very quickly lose their place and feel the stomping of younger feet as the inspired and flexible youth and their teams of like-minded colleagues veritably leap into the leadership roles of the future.

For leaders, becoming comfortable with delegating not only responsibility but the accompanying authority, is proving to be substantially difficult, but in truth, they really have little choice if their business ventures are going to continue to be successful.

Conclusion

Before you are a leader, success is all about growing yourself. When you become a leader,
success is all about growing others.

~ Jack Welch

Tips for Leaders

Share Information: Communicate the news that you can, so minds don't wander and wonder.

Adjust Your Style: There are many different communication styles and personalities on your team. You can no longer manage everyone the same way. In addition, don't assume everyone likes to be managed the way you like to be managed.

Have Fun: You team wants to enjoy going to work. Create opportunities for play.

Do Whatever Needs to be Done: When your people see you putting in extra hours, they are inspired to jump in and follow your lead.

Say Thanks: People want to feel appreciated. A simple Thank You note doesn't cost a thing and makes a huge difference.

Remove Obstacles: Bureaucracy stifles creativity and innovation. Wherever possible, cut down some of the paperwork.

Empower through Delegation: We know no one can do it as well as you can, but you need to give yourself time to complete tasks more appropriate to your position.

Focus Your Time: It's the old 80-20 principle: focus the majority of your time and attention on the 20% of your people and projects that generate 80% of your results.

Set Small Milestones: If you can't match last year's numbers, set milestones that can be reached.

Give Feedback: Your people want and need feedback, and it's crucial in making your team as productive as possible.

"There are many benefits that stem from having a multigenerational team, and to take advantage of these benefits, one must keep these generational differences in mind. Multigenerational teams are known to be more flexible, gain and maintain more market share because they reflect the multigenerational market, make better decisions because of a broader base of knowledge from multiple perspectives, and demonstrate increased creativity and innovation."

~ Adapted from Douglas Magazine, Kerry Slavens, 2016

- Leadership carries a huge responsibility. It requires self-confidence grown through self-awareness. Without confidence, there is no leadership.

- Leaders birth ideas and must be able to weight the merits of them without personal bias. Just because they have an idea doesn't mean it is a good one, and it can be easy to lose sight of that.

- Leaders are only leaders because others are willing to follow them.

- Leaders must never lose sight of the big picture but also be aware that the devil is in the details.

- Leaders can no longer be egocentric; today's workforce will not tolerate the hierarchical structures of the past.

- Leaders must understand how to motivate; this is a much more complex task than it seems.

- Leaders must always lead charismatically through presence, power, and warmth.

- Leaders must excel at change management not only for the desired result of the project or company, but to assist others dealing with unsolicited and undesired upheaval.

- Leaders must practice excellent self-care; others are depending on them.

- Leaders must promote and encourage excellence in others; the best leaders have mentored others to take over the reins in his/her absence.

- Leaders must recognize when it is time to step away and pass the responsibility on to others.

In January of 2017, Forbes shared the following thoughts regarding the individuals making up the largest part of our workforce:

"Their needs and skills are relevant to shaping the future of any business. They've already had an impact on leadership by asking for more transparency and collaboration from managers, and studies show that (they) would like even more feedback than they currently receive. The more feedback they're able to learn from now, the better equipped they'll be to handle that future when they're the boss. Moreover, by receiving feedback that's structured well, they'll also learn how to become coaches to others in the organization."

Regardless of the generation, everyone wants to feel included, and have their ideas acknowledged and feel appreciated. Build on that as a foundation, base your decisions on the desired goals, build a strong business culture, and use the strengths of each of the individuals in your charge.

Leadership does not come with a job description or a set of rules. It will pose challenges, it will be difficult, it will undoubtedly be frustrating at times, and meeting the needs of employees will continue to become much more time consuming.

Modern business demands that leaders understand how to motivate, how to lead through involvement, and how to encourage and reward innovative thinking.

Have the fundamental rules of leadership changed with the generations?

Yes, and no, but regardless of the generation, regardless of the situation, and regardless of preferred method of leadership, the same governing tenet still prevails: Everyone wants to feel included and have their ideas acknowledged and feel appreciated.

Business leaders of the 21st century need to understand that the generations comprising today's workforce are motivated by different values. They must know how to tap into the strengths of each of the groups, they must address their responsibility to mentor and create new leaders, and they must bridge the gaps between the generations so the entire group can work together as a successful, cohesive unit.

Rosemarie Barnes is an internationally acclaimed speaker known for her ability to connect with her audiences in a charismatic and powerful way. Her Bridging the Gaps workshops are in great demand and consistently leave participants with the desire and the tools to ease generational misconceptions and promote maximum engagement in the workplace.

Rosemarie would love to hear your stories of cross generational challenges and successes in the workplace. As a thank you for sharing your story with her, Rosemarie is pleased to offer a 20% discount off 2 tickets to her next available Bridging the Gap Workshop.

Simply mention the discount in the story correspondence addressed to
rbarnes@confidentstages.com

If you would like to have Rosemarie speak at an event, provide a break-out session, or lead a workshop for your business or conference, please contact her office:

rbarnes@confidentstages.com